Promoting racial harmony

The years 1965–8 were the 'liberal hour' for race relations policy in Britain. Laws were then enacted, enforcement agencies created, and community relations councils established. These bodies, and their personnel, have been called 'the race relations industry'. To many people, the output of this 'industry' appears disappointing relative to the input into it. This book examines a variety of possible reasons for low output: failures on the part of the personnel; over-optimistic assumptions about the speed with which immigrants adjust to a new environment; inadequate minority bargaining power; insufficiently speedy and decisive action by the central government; unwillingness on the part of the white majority to accept the desirability of such action; and the difficulty of fitting a race relations policy into an administrative system created to serve an ethnically homogeneous population.

The policies initiated in 1965 reflected the ascendancy of liberal over conservative assumptions about race relations. Now these are under sharp attack from a radical standpoint. *Promoting Racial Harmony* shows how the debate has changed, drawing upon recent economic theory to formulate the issues in an original but non-technical manner.

Promoting racial harmony

MICHAEL BANTON
Professor of Sociology, University of Bristol

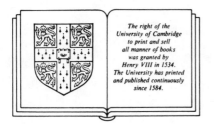

The right of the
University of Cambridge
to print and sell
all manner of books
was granted by
Henry VIII in 1534.
The University has printed
and published continuously
since 1584.

CAMBRIDGE UNIVERSITY PRESS

Cambridge
London   New York   New Rochelle
Melbourne   Sydney

Published by the Press Syndicate of the University of Cambridge
The Pitt Building, Trumpington Street, Cambridge CB2 1RP
32 East 57th Street, New York, NY 10022, USA
10 Stamford Road, Oakleigh, Melbourne 3166, Australia

First published 1985

Printed in Great Britain at the University Press, Cambridge

Library of Congress catalogue card number: 84–14260

British Library cataloguing in publication data

Banton, Michael
Promoting racial harmony
1. Great Britain–Race relations
I. Title
305.8'00941   DA125.A1

ISBN 0 521 30082 7 hard covers
ISBN 0 521 31740 1 paperback

SE

Contents

insufficient to make possible any broadly based mobilization
on the part of Afro-Caribbeans

Preface

There is a brand of cheap humour which thrives on sarcastic references to 'the race relations industry'. The staff of the Commission for Racial Equality and the local Councils for Racial Equality make an easy target for such gibes. It would be unfortunate if this book were seen as lending any support to criticism of this kind for its intent is more serious. Over the past thirty years in Britain there have been a veritable host of committees and associations, official and unofficial, established to promote racial harmony. They have attracted the enthusiasm of many members of the white majority and the various ethnic minorities, people who have been successful in other spheres of their lives and who have worked devotedly for this cause. In comparison with the problems in many other countries, it should be relatively easy to promote racial harmony in Britain, since the majority population is, by international standards, well educated, with a long history of democratic government that has fostered a commitment to ideals of individual freedom, fair-dealing and civility; that population is a secure majority faced by relatively small and unthreatening minorities. Yet most commentators seem to be extremely disappointed with the degree of progress and many of the enthusiasts for the cause have been frustrated by their experiences.

It seems as if the input into organizations for promoting racial harmony has been substantial; the output of actual achievement looks much smaller. That impression is strengthened by the great increase in recent years in the number of specialist teachers employed to promote what is currently called 'multi-cultural' education in schools and by the many appointments of race relations advisers to the staffs of local authorities. It is impossible to decide definitely whether there is such a discrepancy since it is difficult to obtain any satisfactory measure of output, but there is now sufficient information for a discussion of the issues to be worthwhile.

Why is it that the achievements of the race relations industry seem disappointing? Since it is possible to answer this question in many different ways, it is best to begin by classifying the most important kinds of answer.

In the first place, the assumption underlying the question itself can be denied. Perhaps the achievements of the so-called industry have really been very gratifying and observers have failed to realize this because of their failure to examine their own assumptions. They may expect more than is reasonable. They may not appreciate how serious are the obstacles that have to be overcome. Other answers accept, for the purposes of discussion only, that progress seems disappointing, but maintain that it is misleading to write of the 'race relations industry'. The expression was coined originally with a satirical and critical intent (Killian, 1979). In reality there is no industry at all. There are various sorts of people employed by the Commission for Racial Equality, by central and local government departments, people working in a voluntary capacity on local councils or simply members of the public who want to prevent discrimination and promote racial harmony. They work in the circumstances of their own time and place, for which they are not themselves responsible. Any evaluation of organized attempts to promote racial harmony over the last twenty years must distinguish the component parts of the enterprise and consider them separately.

A second kind of answer is that the people engaged in this enterprise have not gone about it very well at either the local or central level. They have quarrelled among themselves about matters of marginal relevance instead of getting on with the job. A third answer is that attempts to promote good relations cannot produce quick results because the immigrants need time to adjust to their new social environment. Progress will be more rapid when the members of all the ethnic minorities have decided that their future lies in Britain and have accepted that, if they wish to change any features of British society, they must work within its framework while seeking their objectives. These considerations lead on to a fourth possible response: that the failure has been one of central direction (or the lack of it) on the part of the sequence of agencies established by parliament from 1965 in order to implement a national strategy. If the staff of these agencies are found wanting they can reply that the responsibility is not theirs alone.

This leads to the fifth answer: that parliament's measures were too little and too late. A central agency should have been created before 1965 and given adequate powers at an earlier stage. To this charge the politicians have a ready answer, for had the government taken action that was too far in advance of what the electors thought necessary they could have lost their seats at the next election. Anyone who wants to blame the government for failure to promote racial harmony more vigorously must be prepared to say what he or she would have done in such circumstances. The politician can also enquire, very reasonably, about the standard employed by someone who is disappointed by a lack of progress towards racial harmony. Many social policies are introduced late and, for one reason or another, are only partially effective. Factory inspectors are appointed, but there are still many industrial accidents. Health visitors call at homes, and parents are sometimes prosecuted for child neglect, but it remains a serious problem. People are sentenced for breaking other laws than those against racial discrimination but the number of recorded offences continues to rise. If policies for racial harmony yield only disappointing results, against what other sorts of policy are they being measured?

This, in its turn, leads on to the sixth kind of answer: that progress has been slow because in a new field of social policy which does not fit easily into the existing administrative structure and cuts across departmental boundaries, it takes time to reach agreement upon objectives and to identify the best means for attaining them. One of the leading text books of social policy discusses various case studies: the introduction of family allowances; the creation of the Open University; health centres; detention centres; legislation against atmospheric pollution; and the abolition of National Assistance (Hall, *et al*, 1975). Opinions about the merits and demerits of these innovations all rest upon assumptions about human nature and the lessons of history. Fundamental divergencies about such matters underlie differences in political outlook. Yet the goals that are to be met by the family allowances policy are recognized by people of very different political persuasion and the scheme is accepted as an efficient if not perfect means of attaining those goals. There may be widespread sympathy with Roy Jenkins' formulation of the goal for racial relations policies as 'equal opportunity accompanied by cultural diversity, in an atmosphere of mutual tolerance' but, very naturally at this stage of events, it is a vaguer conception of the common objective than those which underlie the social policies just mentioned; there is a corresponding lack of certainty about the best means to the end, and therefore any discussion of the issue more readily becomes an exchange of broader political opinions.

There has sometimes been an appearance of racial harmony despite racial inequality. Slaves have seemed content with their condition. New Commonwealth immigrants in Britain in the 1950s took the jobs English people did not want, constituting what some called an under-class or sub-proletariat. They accommodated themselves to the interests of the white majority, and there was little evidence of racial disharmony. But the generation that followed them had higher expectations and were discontent with the lack of equal opportunity. Some Asian minorities presently seek a very considerable measure of cultural diversity. English people can point out that toleration is defined as a forbearance of opinions and practices that are not approved; they can enquire what it is that they are being asked to tolerate and whether it is not preferable to work for a sharing of opinions and practices so that ultimately there is no need for toleration associated with ethnic differences. If harmony stems from a constructive interaction between different viewpoints, may not one source for the disappointment about progress be found in the processes by which people of different political views and people with different cultural values negotiate about those differences in their applications to specific problems?

These six kinds of response to the question are considered, in roughly reverse order, in the chapters which follow.

Abbreviations

BCRE	Bristol Council for Racial Equality
CARD	Campaign Against Racial Discrimination
CRC	Community Relations Commission
CRE	Commission for Racial Equality
CRO	Community Relations Officer
CSD	Civil Service Department
IWA	Indian Workers' Association
NACRC	National Association of Community Relations Councils
NCCI	National Committee for Commonwealth Immigrants
NOAACP	National Organization of African, Asian and Caribbean People
NUT	National Union of Teachers
OPCS	Office of Population Censuses and Surveys
PEP	Political and Economic Planning
RRB	Race Relations Board
VLC	Voluntary Liaison Committee

1

The constraints of nature

Some countries, like Brazil, Mexico, Barbados and Kenya, have multi-racial populations without having a 'race problem', as that expression has conventionally been used. In one sense, racial problems have their origins in people's minds, in their beliefs and assumptions about the significance of differences of skin colour, hair form, and so on. Racial discrimination can be seen as a product of the popular consciousness of racial differences. Since that consciousness takes such different forms from one country to another, any student is obliged to come to some opinion – even if only tacitly – about how such differences arise.

Every scholar and every political activist must work with some philosophy of history, with some set of assumptions, explicit or implicit, coherent or incoherent, as to what is important in human affairs. Those who are Christians may read the historical record as the progressive revelation of God's relationship to his creation. Others may believe that a reader can find lessons in history only because his mind has been taught to look for particular things, or because he is studying a tale which a historian has put together so as to convey the lesson which the historian believes can be deduced from the record. According to this view, people read significance into history and the evidence itself is neutral. Put crudely, it is a philosophy which believes history to be simply 'one damn thing after another'. Those who subscribe to it may be attracted to the conclusion that Edward Gibbon expressed after writing *The Decline and Fall of the Roman Empire*; he said that he could find in history nothing but 'the register of the crimes, follies and misfortunes of mankind'. Part of anyone's philosophy of history will be assumptions about the nature of man and the extent of his freedom to fashion his own future. These assumptions will often be associated with people's political outlooks. A powerful element in the conservative outlook is the belief that it is only natural for men to do evil, a belief that finds vigorous expression in the doctrine of original sin. Radicals, by contrast, have

1

taken over the eighteenth-century romantic tenet that immorality is the product of faulty social organization since man is naturally moral. This leads on to the view that men do not slaughter or brutalize one another unless they are influenced by some ideology which either impels them to behave in this way or furnishes excuses for so doing. The liberals see elements of truth in both these outlooks, but put their stress on the mediating power of institutions. According to this interpretation, United States soldiers would not have slain babies in Vietnam had they not been conditioned to obedience and rendered insensitive to the consequences of their actions. Experiments by social psychologists have indeed demonstrated that ordinary people are prepared to endanger the lives of others when they see the responsibility as lying with the experimenter.

Assumptions of this kind will affect people's opinions about the kind of racial harmony to work for, and the way to do it. A political tactician will want to define an objective so that it is shared by the largest possible number of people, and it was obviously sensible for the Labour government in 1965 to attack racial discrimination as contrary to national ideals. It is not meant as a criticism to call this a negative policy, one aimed simply at eliminating an evil. The government could properly say that once the barriers had been broken down people would be free to form whatever social groups they wished, and it was none of the government's business to say whether they should mix themselves up or remain as separate communities so long as they had the freedom to choose. Others would reply, however, that the historical record shows that people do not easily give up their routines of custom and habit, that social structures set further limits to choice, or that prejudices will remain in the private realm long after discrimination in the public realm has been brought to an end. Some of the alternatives people would choose would prove not to be viable; others look more promising and it is these, so it would be said, that people should be encouraged to select.

Three views of these matters deserve special attention. The first treats popular consciousness of race as the product of human genes; the second as the product of competition between nations; and the third as the product of the capitalist mode of production. The three views have been presented as theories that can be tested in the same sort of way as the theory of natural selection. Such claims are contested, but whatever conclusion be reached about the scientific status of the arguments there is no doubt that they can be used as philosophies of history stressing respectively the predominating influence upon events of the factors of race, nationality and class. To the extent to which anyone is attracted to these views so he or she will see race, nationality or class as an important constraint upon the likely success of any policy for promoting racial harmony.

The racial thesis was propounded in the middle of the nineteenth century in the form of an assertion that there was a limited number of permanent racial types, each with distinctive capacities suited to a particular continent or region of the world. Darwin's demonstration that there were no permanent forms in nature destroyed this claim. A very different version was propounded in 1931, and with great elegance, by the anatomist Sir Arthur Keith. In the course of his rectorial address to the students of the University of Aberdeen, he described what he considered the ingenuity of nature in the original organization of group relations:

> She had arranged it on a competitive basis; each tribe was a team engaged in the eternal struggle to obtain promotion and avoid relegation. Our modern masters of football have but copied the scheme of competition which Nature had set up in her ancient world. Her League of Humanity had its divisions – racial divisions – white, yellow, brown, and black. Tribes constituted her competing teams. No transfers for her; each member of the team had to be home-born and home-bred. She did not trust her players or their managers farther than she could see them! To make certain they would play the great game of life as she intended it should be played she put them into colours – not transferable jerseys, but liveries of living flesh, such liveries as the races of the modern world now wear. She made certain that no player could leave his team without being recognized as a deserter (Keith, 1931: 34–5).

In this vision there are two central propositions. First, though there are many races, nations and regional groups, and occasionally one disappears or gets absorbed by another, the number of these groups is finite. Secondly, to which group or groups any particular individual belongs is determined by the processes of natural selection. Nature is organized for the evolution of new and better races of mankind. Selection can take place because there is variation in the genes inherited among any human population: those genes which are less well adapted to the perpetuation of that group in its particular environment are, over time, eliminated by natural and by sexual selection; other genes are favoured.

The characteristic of a team is that the members share ends, or objectives, and organize their activities so as to attain them. In this sense their ends, or some of them at least, are integrated. According to Keith, integration is achieved by the operation of natural selection, so that while some players may be disloyal and not play hard enough, over the course of time those teams well supplied with the genes that produce team-spirit will be favoured. The obverse side of team-spirit is antagonism towards opposing teams, so that racial and national prejudice are seen as serving an evolutionary function. Racial and national sentiment are only superficially different manifestations of what are represented as underlying biological processes, but since for most people the adjective racial better represents biological processes, Keith's theory can be described as one which declares the constitution and interaction of groups to be a matter of race.

The second philosophy of history's teams takes nation as the key unit. It was first put forward in a modern form by Walter Bagehot in a book entitled *Physics and Politics, or Thoughts on the Application of the Principles of 'Natural Selection' and 'Inheritance' to Political Society*. As the subtitle indicates, Bagehot had been reading Darwin. He concluded that two forces had been responsible for the creation of the major differences between the branches of mankind; during the period of antiquity there had been a race-making force which 'has now wholly, or almost, given over acting', yielding place to the nation-making force (1873: 86). Not all nations progress. From the study of the characteristics of the progressive nations, Bagehot deduced three laws, the first two of which were of most importance:

> First. In every particular state of the world, those nations which are strongest tend to prevail over the others; and in certain marked peculiarities the strongest tend to be the best.
> Secondly. Within every particular nation the type or types of character there and then most attractive tend to prevail; and the most attractive, though with exceptions, is what we call the best character.

Thus Bagehot, like Keith sixty years later, saw human affairs as the product of laws governing the nature of relatively large units. Nation and race could overlap. Membership of such units was, for Bagehot, determined not just by inheritance but by the constraints of geography and history upon nation formation and by the social processes which caused particular types to prevail. These processes included the development of political and legal institutions (for Bagehot had been reading the work of Sir Henry Maine as well) and the ways in which psychological impulses were channelled, particularly the 'unconscious imitation and encouragement of appreciated character', for 'there is always some reason why the fashion of female dress is what it is' (1873: 97, 89). The formation of type, or national character, is therefore both a matter of unconscious national selection and one of 'custom-making' or, in present day speech, of culture. Individual choice is constrained by the wider social processes but, since these reward cooperation, human history can be seen as the progressive development of human capabilities.

A third view acknowledges that teams may appear to be based on racial or national identity but asserts that these appearances are misleading and that ultimately the deciding criterion is that of class. Karl Marx maintained that the players recognize rules governing competition between teams but do not at the outset understand the principles which decide for which teams they should play and who are their true opponents. Initially there are few permanent teams, but gradually it is appreciated that what matters is the process of production and the way that people at different points in ths process share interests in opposition to people at other points; they learn to play for their class. To start with there are lots of classes (Marx referred to eleven in France and Germany in the late 1840s and the list was not meant to be complete), but their number is progressively reduced as the underlying divisions come into view. Sections of the ruling class are precipitated into the proletariat. The small traders of the lower middle class discover that their interests speak against any alliance with the capitalists. So the quarter-finals and semi-finals are fought; cross-cutting ties that bound diverse groups are stripped away until society is polarized and ready for the cup final in which the proletariat is bound to conquer. The capitalists attempt to postpone this day of reckoning by encouraging the production of ideologies which justify the prevailing order and delay the rise of proletarian class consciousness. They seize on the physical differences between populations and the sentiments of solidarity among people sharing common cultures to elaborate doctrines of racism and nationalism.

This answer, like the previous two, contends that while there are many kinds and sizes of groups, one kind is of particular importance in human history. Like them, it accords little importance to bargaining. At any one moment of time the number of such major groups is finite but the number is gradually being reduced as part of a unilinear process. Social classes are not created by the subjective perceptions of individuals looking at the differences of social status between themselves and their neighbours; they are the units of which history is built. Though individuals may be perverse or deluded they are gradually brought to appreciate that their membership in a class is of surpassing importance to them.

The 'theories' of Keith, Bagehot and Marx are, among other things, attempts to account for the course of history. They assert that among the many factors which influence what happens in history, one particular kind of grouping tends to dominate the others. There are, of course, serious difficulties in the path of any such argument if it is expressed in such simple terms. On the one hand, since human history is unique it is impossible to prove the truth of claims about its determining forces. On the other, it is impracticable to separate factors like pieces in a jigsaw puzzle. The racial idiom has been powerful in the West because it was launched in the nineteenth century as a way of explaining the pre-eminence in world affairs attained by peoples originating in Western Europe, and it was the more plausible because 'race' was used in a way that overlapped with 'nation'. In other parts of the world today, such as in Southern Africa, race is often thought to overlap with class. While stressing the significance of class formation, the classic Marxist writers like Lenin accepted nations as natural groupings; they would have considered any attempt to compare the relative significance of national and class sentiment as misconceived.

Philosophies which see race, nation, class or some other kind of grouping as having a special influence upon the course of history all look at history in the long term. Those who subscribe to such views accept that in the short term a multitude of other factors influence behaviour. In pursuit of their private objectives individuals form an infinite number of groups of very varied character; some of them, like the institutions of government for example, are relatively permanent so that each new generation is constrained by structures created by its predecessors. They in their turn strengthen or weaken features of these institutions so that there is a continuing process in which groups are formed, maintained and dissolved. Social scientists study many aspects of this process. Psychologists, for example, have learned a great deal about perception, memory, personality patterns and how these interact with social conditions. Economists have constructed a sophisticated conceptual structure for analysing the implications of different kinds of decision about the allocation of scarce resources. Political analysts have their techniques for examining public opinion and calculating its relevance to electoral programmes. The list is a long one. What should be stressed at this point is that social scientists can obtain a kind of knowledge about the things they study which is of a different order from most kinds of historical knowledge.

Social scientists can to some extent control the variables influencing the things that are of interest to them. Sometimes they can experiment. Quite often they can, if they wish, measure the objects of their study, either by using an accepted criterion, such as money value, or by devising a special scale. They may be able to advance their understanding by comparing what happened in one set of circumstances with what happened in another. They can do this because their objective is not to obtain an exhaustive understanding of what they study but only to understand certain features which are of particular significance in the light of the theory or theories they are seeking to test, apply, or extend. This reduces the influence of subjective judgement and makes it possible for one research worker to try to replicate another's findings. The checking of others' findings occurs in the historical field also, and in view of the great variety of historical study it is unwise to make more than a modest claim for the distinction. In some fields within history, particularly in the earlier periods, factual information is limited and offers little scope for alternative reconstructions, but the general characteristics of historical writing are its chronological rather than theoretical framework, and the breadth of its criteria of relevance. All sorts of considerations can be relevant to understanding why a particular event took place, why it assumed a particular form and had particular consequences. The greater the breadth of focus the more the resulting knowledge is affected by subjective perceptions and reconstructions. From this standpoint the distinction can be seen as a continuous scale. At the end are psychological experiments of a kind that could equally well be carried out in biological science laboratories and which yield what may be called positive knowledge. At the other end are broad historical surveys which for their character depend very much upon the interests and sensitivities of their authors. For other purposes it can be helpful to think of the distinctions as relating to different levels of knowledge, though there is much disagreement about the nature of these levels and the relations between them.

Evolutionary theories, like that of Sir Arthur Keith, represent human behaviour as the product of causes operating on several different levels. The highest level is that of culture, the realm which organizes the interpretations that people place upon their experience and which vests different kinds of behaviour with special meanings. The forms taken by culture are influenced by their environments and in particular by the economic organization which enables people to exploit the natural resources around them, so one or more levels underneath the cultural one may be distinguished in the effort to identify the ecological causes of behaviour. The ability of humans to utilize their environment depends in part upon their psychological make-up, their intelligence, learning power and ability to make the most of their inherited potential – which includes their physical constitution; one or more levels can be added to take account of these. The psychology and zoology of *homo sapiens* can be seen as the product of the nature and distribution of human genes, which in turn are constituted from biochemical components. Evolutionary explanations maintain that some, but not all, of the observations made at each level can be accounted for by the principles used to explain observations at the next level down. This is usually called a reductionist explanation because it reduces the problems of one level to those of the next by reformulating them in terms of the concepts used at the lower level. Thus the disapproval of sexual relations defined as incestuous may be explained as the expression of a biological imperative to avoid in-breeding. Yet even so, certain unexplained questions remain, such as: why should legislatures find it necessary to enact laws against incest and why should the definition of forbidden relationships vary from one society to another? The unexplained observations are called the remainder. How big the remainder is varies from case to case, but reductionists are inclined to believe that as scientific knowledge grows the remainders at every level are progressively diminished. They see their theory as scientific, as based upon and yielding positive knowledge, in contrast to the subjectivist approach of conventional historians.

The chief modern exponent of Keith's view is Pierre L. van den Berghe, a sociologist in the United States; he has elaborated it at some length, employing concepts taken from socio-biology. Kinship is of central importance, for if people help their kin they are helping the genes which they share with their kinsfolk to survive and to increase in future generations. In this way the willingness of people to help their kinsfolk is said to be genetically determined. Ethnicity can be seen as an extension of kinship and accounted for in a similar manner, racial prejudice being regarded as a positive feature because it helps each group develop its genetic distinctiveness. The argument cannot be faulted on logical grounds but there is little evidence about just how much behaviour at each level can be explained in terms of the influences operating at the next level down, and good reason to suspect that the remainder at each level is far too substantial for any reductionist theory to be, on present information, any more than a set of hypotheses that require many years of detailed investigations before they become relevant to the discussion of social problems.

Bagehot's theory was an evolutionary one, but he maintained that what would now be called the genetic determinants were of little power compared to the psychological and social forces enabling nations to mobilize political power. This concern with the nation as a social unit of special significance has been given extra significance in recent times by the creation of so many new states and by the attempts of some ethnic groups inside states to be recognized as independent nations. One who shares the concern is Mr Enoch Powell, though he may well see the existence of nations as part of the working out of God's purpose for mankind. For him, a nation must be independent; its members must be willing to die for it; they must have a consciousness and a conviction of belonging together and of being at one with their forebears who defended the territory they have inherited. Nations which fail to recognize the conditions for their existence disintegrate, and no other large social unit can bind people together so effectively.

In nineteenth-century writing, nation and race were often inter-changeable words. For a group to be considered a nation it had to have a territory so that a state could be established to govern that territory in accordance with the wishes of the nation. In the twentieth century there have been attempts to fashion a sense of national identification based upon the possession of a common culture rather than a common territory. Such an enterprise has obvious relevance to Afro-Americans who are a population greater than that of Norway, Sweden, Denmark and the Netherlands combined. In Britain the argument is often advanced in discussion that racial harmony cannot be attained on the terms of white people who regard a black or brown complexion as a misfortune. For there to be harmony there must first be equal dignity. Black and brown people must be able to identify contentedly with some bigger culture-bearing social unit just as white people do. Thus it has been asserted that adoption agencies must seek to place children for adoption with adoptive parents who have the same racial and cultural origins as the child, thus maintaining an identification of race with culture in spite of the general recognition that culture is transmitted by learning (see *The Guardian*, 26 January 1983). This sounds like a kind of cultural nationalism which could contend that racial harmony requires a recognition of the United Kingdom as a multi-national state containing not only an English, Welsh, Scottish nation but also a black and possibly one or more Asian nations (what the status of Northern Ireland would be in such a scheme is a further problem throwing another light onto the problem of group definition).

Marx took many of his philosophical ideas from Hegel, who believed that while men could acquire positive knowledge by experimental methods they could also gain access to a more comprehensive knowledge by locating observations in an understanding of human development. Marxist writers generally assume that the realm of historical knowledge is superior to that of positive knowledge for the pursuit of what Westerners call social science. According to this view, any uniformities discovered by psychologists, economists and political scientists are valid only for particular historical epochs. Even more important is the principle that any research worker in these fields should first understand the laws of social development so that he can act like a midwife to history in hastening the advance of the progressive forces. He or she should select a research topic with this aim in mind. This view does not allow for the possibility that the research worker might discover that the alleged laws of development are wrong. For all important purposes the traffic goes in one direction alone. It can be useful to view the ferment in modern Western Marxism as reaction against such propositions. Marx only claimed that the social superstructure was brought into line with the economic base in periods of revolution; in between such periods political and cultural institutions could enjoy a relative autonomy. Moreover there is room for argument about whether even this proposition should be treated like an article of faith. Many of those who draw inspiration from Marx' writings would reject any one-way view of the relations between historical and positive knowledge, insisting that by their research they can improve upon Marx' understanding of historical change.

Contemporary sociologists who stand in the Marxist tradition (e.g. Miles, 1982) have brought a special force to the argument that no scholarly study of the conflicts between groups identified by race can take for granted popular beliefs about the nature and significance of racial differences. If sociologists are to write about racial groups they must base their conception of race upon something more secure and precise than the vague and shifting assumptions of popular consciousness. However, simply to maintain that the underlying forces are those of class formation is inadequate in view of the special characteristics of racial politics. When racial features are used to identify and enforce differences of status this introduces a greater rigidity than is found in class politics. Status is transmitted from one generation to another and social mobility blocked in a more comprehensive and inescapable way. The range of alternatives open to an individual appears to be subject to an additional constraint. Where racial identifications become a basis for political alignment the normal processes of democratic politics as these are understood in the West are undermined because there is then no floating vote (the instance of Northern Ireland shows that this feature of racial politics is not limited to situations in which political alignment is associated with physical difference). An important feature of the democratic process is that groups with different objectives and of different political strength negotiate with one another. But when the rights of a group are protected by the constitution (as in the disputes over French Canadian rights and over the electoral privileges of whites in Zimbabwe) its members may refuse to negotiate because any revision of the original settlement is certain to reduce their rights. The belief that class is ultimately the most important influence is no more vulnerable to disproof than the corresponding beliefs about race and nation and it may furnish no solution to the analysis of problems in the short and medium term.

Different views about human nature and the lessons of history structure peoples' ideas about what kind of racial harmony is possible and what are the conditions that permit its growth. The oppositions between some of the contending arguments discussed in later chapters have their origins in differences of this kind. Yet in other areas of social policy (like the six cases mentioned in the Preface) conflicts of political philosophy have not prevented the introduction of new policies. Perhaps it is more difficult for the various parties concerned about policies for racial harmony to negotiate with one another about their differences? The next chapter therefore descends from abstract level of dispute about the interpretation of history to discuss the means used by groups when they seek to advance their shared interests.

2

The realm of action

Harmony, in racial as in industrial relations, is a product of bargaining. Almost every kind of social relation includes an element of bargaining. It is most explicit in the market place where people bargain consciously over the price of goods. There is every reason to believe that the spread of market relations, in which price relates demand to supply, has been a critical element in economic growth around the world during the past 300 years or so, since it has made possible the great increase in consumer demand. But bargaining is not limited to the market place for there is a great range of relations in which a more diffuse kind of haggling occurs which encompasses more than can be expressed in monetary terms: someone invited to be manager of a football team, chairman of a government committee or secretary of a local social club may be willing to do the job only on his or her own terms (like the degree of independence to be allowed), and this, too, is a form of bargaining. Similarly, political parties compete for the votes of particular sections of the electorate, calculating how far they can afford to go in order to attract their support. There may be general agreement that some things are not to be bought and sold in the market place, such as those affecting life and health, but it is often difficult to draw a line; there has, for example, been a serious debate about whether supplies of blood for transfusion are better allocated by a system of voluntary donation or by market principles. Occasionally people are forced, against their will, to bargain about services they believe should be supplied outside the market. Sometimes people may not admit to others, or perhaps even to themselves, that their decisions are influenced by calculations of whether the incentive they are being offered makes it worthwhile for them to do what is being asked of them, although more cynical onlookers may believe that their behaviour reflects such calculations.

In a book called *Racial and Ethnic Competition* the author has argued that competition between groups tends to harden the boundaries between them and reduce the possibilities of inter-group harmony, whereas competition on an individual basis tends to dissolve the boundaries between the groups to which the parties belong. Individual competition, or bargaining, is therefore preferable. It is not always practicable. The most fateful example of group bargaining today is that over nuclear weapons. Some individuals in the West wish all nuclear weapons dismantled but they cannot contract out of the negotiations between the two major power blocks. In industrial relations people frequently have little choice about which trade union or employers' association will represent them: there is a pattern of group bargaining which reflects structures that constrain the liberties of individual participants. The efficiency of such bargaining procedures is of the greatest importance. In disarmament negotiations this is obvious. In industrial relations the pressure of union demands can contribute significantly to increased output. Economic growth may be less rapid when people fail to recognize an opportunity to bargain, when they are prevented from bargaining effectively (as black labour in South Africa has been handicapped) or when miscalculation leads to an excessive number of disputes.

When one party is prevented from bargaining effectively, or is unable to bargain at all, there may be an appearance of harmony, but in the long run harmony is possible only when the parties accept the relationship as fair. The parties do not have to be equal. Bargaining occurs because people have different wants, have different goods or services to trade, and belong to different kinds of bargaining units. The previous chapter made use of an analogy between social groups and football teams. Any sporting team consists of a collection of individuals who cooperate in pursuit of the shared aims of recreation and, usually, of victory over an opposing team. Social groups can also be seen as comprised of individuals who find it better to combine to seek their private ends, some of which they share with other members of the group. The number of shared aims that can bring individuals together in this way is infinite, yet in any particular situation the individual may have scarcely any alternative but to identify himself or herself with one particular group. The more group identification helps an individual attain his or her ends, the harder will the individual work on that group's behalf.

The ends of individuals may be integrated by economic necessity so as to form a social group. For example, in many pre-industrial agrarian economies land was owned and worked by family units. To manage the farm the household had to be relatively large with sons continuing to reside under the family roof after marriage. All its members were dependent upon the family land and what it could produce; there were no state benefits for the sick or unemployed. The other members were subject to the authority of the father because he controlled the use of the land; he and his wife could decide when they would retire and hand it over to the next generation, and how the patrimony would then be divided. Until that time the other members had to rely upon the father's ability as a manager in trying to get the best yield, and upon the mother's skill in managing the household. The younger generations were subject to their authority because all were dependent upon the group and its success both in producing for the market (or in subsistence) and in competing with similar groups for status in the local community. Children were socialized to a cultural pattern based upon such units so they looked to the family group for support and felt morally obliged to help other family members. Identification with a group derives from the expectation both of economic reward in pursuing material ends and of psychological reward in seeking the emotional satisfaction fashioned by cultural processes.

Competition between farming households has taken a special form in Hindu India where the individual's ends are integrated with those of fellow members in a series of groups: in the household; in the wider kin group; in the *jati* (or sub-caste) comprising all the descent group of a particular status possessing the right to practise a particular occupation; and in larger village, regional, linguistic or religious groups. One family unit competes with other such units within the same *jati* to gain *izzat* (prestige) by making the most advantageous marriages; *jatis* compete with one another over relative rank; loyalties to kin and caste come first and there is little recognition of any wider public interest. Because high-caste people are dependent upon low-caste people to perform services they consider polluting, and the complex division of labour makes different *jatis* dependent on each other, cooperation is enforced by circumstance. The pursuit of purely private interests does not have the deleterious consequences that would arise in most other kinds of social system.

In a game of football only one team can win. In the theory of games this is said to be a 'zero-sum' game for the extent of one team's victory is the extent of the other's defeat, and the two outcomes add up to zero (because they cancel each other out). But in so far as the players are concerned to enjoy the game, and some of them can do so even though their side loses, this is a 'positive-sum' situation. The total satisfactions of all the players adds up to something greater than would have been the case had the game not been played. Some kinds of competition, such as that between *jatis* for prestige, resemble zero-sum games. If, say, representatives of the formerly low-ranking Noniya *jati* succeed in persuading others that because of the misfortunes that befell them at the time of the Mogul invasion their true status has been misunderstood and that they are really of Kshatriya rank, coming above, say, the weavers and the money-lenders, then the number of places they move up the caste hierarchy equates with the number of places other *jatis* move down. They cancel each other out. Other kinds of competition resemble positive-sum games, in that they provide stimuli that increase total output.

The analogy of the football game draws attention to the way that competition is regulated by rules. A team that regularly breaks the rules may be suspended or excluded from future contests. In the industrial field competition may be regulated by government legislation designed to ensure fair trading. Members of different *jatis* may hate one another but still feel that it would be wrong to kill one another. Though there can be no sharp distinction between the two, it can be useful to distinguish competition, as a form of struggle conducted according to rules, from conflict, as a kind of struggle in which no rules are recognized. Such rules may be observed when there is a superior power prepared to enforce them. Members of a group may also be tempted to ignore the rules in dealing with a weaker competitor but believe that this would be a dangerous precedent when they in turn have to face a stronger group. Zero-sum competition between groups is less likely to be dangerous in a social system composed of many groups of comparable power, particularly when it is easy for two weak groups to support each other against a stronger. This kind of competition can be dangerous when there is an imbalance of power, and no group's history illustrates this better than the Jews. They have sought recognition both of the right to compete in the market place as individuals and of the right to be a separate intermarrying religious community. They have learned what might be called the Jewish lesson: that if they are to enjoy their right to a separate identity as a minority, they must support the claims of other minorities to a similar right.

The combination of individual competition in the market place with group organization in private relations poses particular problems because the legal systems suited to individual competition have difficulty recognizing any group rights in contradistinction to the sharing of rights by individuals. Preferential policies guaranteeing a quota of places to particular minorities are not easy to formulate or administer. Affirmative action policies in the United States have often benefited other kinds of individuals than those they were intended to help.

Physically distinguishable minorities have from time to time experienced genocidal attacks or have been expelled from territories in which they had rights of residence, as Asians were expelled from East Africa at the end of the 1960s. These incidents have come about when there has been an imbalance of power, a lack of shared interests and ties bringing together the opposed groups, and no superior power to enforce rules of competition.

The social and political systems of different countries offer different opportunities and different protections to minority groups so that Chinese in Jamaica and Guyana, Japanese in Brazil and Canada, Indians in Guyana and Fiji, Jamaicans in New York and London, have developed into different kinds of minority group despite their similarities of origin and appearance. Non-Hindu minorities in India have found that the expectations of people accustomed to a caste system are so strong that their groups have been forced to adopt the characteristics of a *jati*. Sometimes the dominant group allows members of an immigrant minority to qualify for the occupations practised by its own members and raises no barriers to intermarriage; sometimes it acts so as to keep minority members in subordinate roles. The intensity and character of the prejudice members of one group express towards members of another can be explained much better in terms of the way the social system channels their interests than by referring to a supposed inherited disposition of the kind posited by Sir Arthur Keith.

In some areas of social life elaborate systems of bargaining have been developed, the best known being those for regulating workers' claims for better pay and conditions of work. Bargaining about these issues in capitalist countries has been possible because technological advances have led to increased profit, trade unions have secured legal rights to represent their members and workers have won or retained the right to withdraw their labour. The union's threat to call a strike has usually been more powerful than the management's threat to impose a lock-out. The exchange of threats opens up the possibility of a negative-sum game in which both parties are worse off as a result of the action taken. The main drive behind bargaining, however, has been the attraction of a positive-sum outcome. This arises because the management is rarely free to change conditions of work just as it wishes in order to respond to changed circumstances, and the employees have to be offered some incentive to change their working practices. The incidence of 'go slow' or 'work to rule' actions is an indication of how rules which seem sensible at the time they were introduced may be reduced to bargaining counters on a later occasion. There are also a host of respects in which management may be insufficiently well informed about how great a value workers place upon, say, improved holiday rights and about the priority they attach to these compared with better medical benefits when they are sick. The workers' representatives may be ill informed about some of the constraints upon management arising from the markets in which they sell the produce or from current technological changes. Bargaining about these matters can therefore include (i) a zero-sum element: what proportion of an increased profit is to be distributed in increased wages; (ii) a positive-sum element: to what extent will, say, new incentives result in higher production in the future; (iii) a communication element: does the bargaining process itself inform the parties about the implications of their present wishes so that they reorder their priorities and enter the next round of negotiations with more realistic objectives, thus increasing the chances of success? The bargaining is given extra impetus by the possibility of (iv) a negative-sum element: the fear of wrecking action based on the belief that 'it will hurt us more than it will hurt them' or the frustration that produces an overwhelming desire to hurt the other side.

Wage negotiations have been analysed in detail by economists who have been able to deduce certain principles applicable to all bargaining relations. One of these is the notion of commitment. Two bargainers meet: each has an idea of what the other might agree to and the limit at which he would stop negotiating and take action of another kind. For example, the union representative may regard a wage increase of 5p per hour as the minimum that he can accept, but believe that management could afford to concede 10p per hour. The management negotiator may believe that the workforce would not strike providing wages are increased by at least 3p, and be under instruction from the company to concede no more than 8p. There is then a range from 5p to 8p at which both parties are ready to settle. If the union negotiator were to address a meeting of his members and commit himself to obtaining 7p, saying that he would resign if he failed to do so, this would put pressure on the management negotiator to conclude that he would have to settle between 7p and 8p unless he could offer the union negotiator something else (like holiday rights) which would enable him to accept, say, 6p, and still maintain that he had honoured his commitment. The company could, of course, also utilize commitment tactics by taking up a public stand on some item which was part of the union's demands. Commitment can be a risky business (most obviously seen in bargaining over disarmament); for while, if successful, it can give one party an advantage, if unsuccessful it makes that party's position much more difficult than it otherwise would have been.

Another tactic which can be utilized is for the union officials to resign and, in the United States, perhaps even to stop collecting union subscriptions or 'dues'. They threaten the management that unless the company deals with them and takes their demands seriously, the workers will either join some more aggressive union or the management will have to contend with a dissatisfied and under-productive workforce likely to turn the position into a negative-sum situation for lack of an informed leadership. These circumstances have an obvious parallel in some cases of inter-racial bargaining. Minority representatives may say 'unless you deal with us we will be unable to restrain our young men who are very angry'. In these circumstances it may still be useful to see the majority and the minority as involved in a bargaining relationship, despite the absence of any agent or agency to bargain on behalf of the minority.

It may be helpful to emphasize what is entailed in a bargaining relationship. In the market place buyers and sellers bargain when there is a range of prices at which the parties would be willing to settle but frequently those parties have to think about future transactions. If one drives too-hard a bargain the other may seek to trade with someone else on future occasions. In some circumstances, too, a bargain can be undone if the goods do not come up to expectations. If one of the parties is powerful, either because of the prospect of future favours or because of his power in other spheres, he may insist on the revision of the terms of a bargain after the event. Negotiations over wages are often influenced by the way the parties are bound into a continuing relationship. Nor is this simply a relationship between two parties. Negotiators on behalf of the management may represent several employers and those on the other side represent several unions. The negotiators are often involved in bargaining relations with those whom they represent. In a struggle over a wage claim, some union members may be unwilling to strike and ready to accept whatever the employers offer; some may want to fight for unrealistic demands; some will trust their representative and others will not. The representative's power to bargain with the employers is weakened either if there is a likelihood of most workers accepting the employers' terms or of most workers' refusing to accept any offer the employers are willing to make. The representative's power to bargain with the employers is increased if he can force recalcitrant members of either extreme persuasion to abide by the bargain he has struck on their behalf.

In industrial relations most people identify themselves with the management or with the employees as a body, and usually the union or unions represent the latter. Very few cannot identify with either side; very few opt out. Yet many employees are reluctant to carry their psychological identification to the point of supporting a union financially or by attending meetings in their free time. This gives rise to what is called the 'free-rider' problem, an expression apparently coined in labour union circles in the United States. One of the difficulties of union officials is that if, by bargaining with the management, they secure a wage increase for all employees in a particular category, the benefits are enjoyed by union members and non-members alike. A non-union employee who set out to calculate whether it was worthwhile joining the union would ascertain what it would cost to pay the subscriptions or dues required. Then he would work out the extent to which the union's power to win a wage rise was increased by his joining. Next he would compare the likely benefit of his joining with the cost of doing so. Usually he would conclude that his economic interest was not to join but instead to take a 'free-ride' at the expense of his fellow employees who bore the costs of supporting the union. In *The Logic of Collective Action* (1965) Mancur Olson generalizes this by showing that in a whole range of situations rational self-interested individuals will not act to advance their common interests. Profit-maximizing firms in a perfectly competitive industry can be led by the logic of their situation to act in ways that are contrary to their interests as a group. Nor is it necessarily rational for them to sacrifice time and money to support a lobbying organization to seek government assistance for the industry. Marx was wrong to suggest that workers would be led by self-interest alone to organize on a class basis. It was Lenin who was right for he emphasized the communist's need to rely on a self-sacrificing and disciplined minority rather than upon the common interests of the collective mass. For the same reason collective action by members of an ethnic group will not be generated solely by shared interest (see Hechter, Friedman and Appelbaum, 1982).

There are plenty of instances which do not fit in with this theory and suggest that there must be something wrong with it. Individuals do get together in pursuit of shared interests. Manufacturers combine to fix prices, restrict production and create pressure groups. Trade unions often acquire great power, and class-based political parties are scarcely unusual. Olson replies that the membership and power of large pressure-group organizations does not derive in the first instance from their lobbying achievements but is instead a by-product of their other activities. Early trade unions attracted members by providing 'friendly society' benefits ranging from dispute and unemployment payments to sickness and superannuation schemes. They instituted special in-surance arrangements, handled individual grievances and provided recreational services. Having gained a significant membership they could then press for a closed shop. The struggle for union power was marked by violence directed against free riders. Olson quotes research suggesting that though over 90 per cent of trades unionists will not attend meetings or participate in union affairs, the same proportion will vote for a closed shop, forcing themselves to belong and pay subscrip-tions because they sense that this is the only way to overcome their own inclination to take a free ride; this, too, is economically rational. They commit themselves in a way that restricts their future freedom and by so doing increase their bargaining power.

The likelihood of collective organization depends significantly upon the opportunities for minorities within those collectivities to obtain positions of power in which they can create new alternatives for their fellow members and change the relative attractiveness of different alternatives. They manipulate the situation so that rational actors come to a different result when they calculate where their best interests lie. Seen from this standpoint, the existence of races, nations and classes cannot be taken for granted. The readiness of individuals to identify themselves with such groups has to be explained in terms of the value the individuals place upon the benefits they receive from these groups whether they be of a material or an emotional kind. It has also to be explained in terms of the alternative identifications open to them, for the range of options is constrained by the circumstances of geographical location, historical moment, economic and political power, and so forth. (As the reader will readily expect, many objections have been raised against this way of accounting for human behaviour. It has inspired a substantial and highly technical literature, which demonstrates that even its critics believe it worth detailed examination.)

Since this perspective will be utilized in subsequent chapters, two further comments on the free-rider problem are necessary. Firstly, it is misleading to see this as a feature of the short-term calculation of individual interest without allowing for the ability of people to appreciate that if everyone tries to take a free-ride no one gets a ride at all. Philosophers have distinguished between 'act utilitarianism' in which individuals act so as to maximize their utility and 'rule utilitarianism' in which they formulate rules which, when enforced, enable them to maximize their utility. For example, by voting for a closed shop workers establish a rule which should serve their long term interest by preventing free-riding (see also Harsanyi, 1982: 57–8). Secondly, the free-rider has his complement in the person who is an unwilling rider, the captive traveller. This is the group member who feels obliged to conform to the behaviour expected by fellow members of his group even though he believes it contrary to his, and perhaps the group's, long-term interest. The value which the actor places on group approval is greater than that he might otherwise obtain, since, even if he might eventually bring about a change in group attitudes the disapproval he would incur while agitating for the change would be prohibitive. Group loyalty of this kind can be vital in racial, national and class conflicts.

It is finally worth recalling Olson's claim that the capacity of an association to act as a pressure group is usually a by-product of relations established with a different objective. This is particularly relevant to the understanding of ethnic collective action in situations of immigration. It helps explain why the strength of ties built up prior to migration, like those of kinship and congregational organizations based on synagogue, mosque or temple, is so important to collective action in the new country. Pre-migration institutional patterns are a kind of social capital making it possible for individuals to draw upon their credit with fellow group members in times of difficulty or when creating new groups. A minority with a range of strong primary groups can pursue shared economic interests much more effectively than another minority lacking those groups even though the second minority may seem objectively much more disadvantaged and with more cause to solve its problems by collective action.

Inter-racial bargaining in Britain is not institutionalized like industrial negotiating; perhaps it never can be and never should be, but the parallels are still illuminating. Spokesmen for the minorities cannot enter into bargains on behalf of those they claim to represent; they have no power to make them stand by an agreement even if it should be endorsed by most members of the minority, for, unlike union leaders, they have no legal standing, control no funds, and cannot expel members who misbehave. Though people may change their jobs those who are on the management side tend to stay on that side; employees tend to stay employees. Ethnic minority members are not involved in so stable a relationship because they are caught up in processes of assimilation originating in the majority society, even if they struggle against those processes. Their attitudes towards the majority change according to the issue and they change over time. The number of possible teams on the minority side is infinite, since each individual can go his or her own way. There is therefore little direct bargaining between the ethnic minorities and the majority. The main struggles are within the minorities, and centre upon attempts to create bargaining agencies. These struggles within the minorities turn upon their shared relations with the majority and therefore involve different sections of opinion within the majority.

For an immigrant minority to establish a bargaining agency, especially a minority that has not brought an institutional structure with it, is very difficult – but difficult by comparison with what? People with shared interests in the majority population cannot easily pursue those interests unless they can form a pressure group and persuade one or more political groups to take up their cause. The political process can be seen as one of bargaining in which parties sacrifice some of their objectives in order to obtain others which are of greater value to them. In parliament or the county or district council the majority party (having arranged its preferences in an order of priority) can reach decisions which are binding upon everyone within their jurisdiction, whether they voted for that party or not. No one can contract out of paying taxes or rates in the way in which they can refrain from supporting an organization that seeks to promote racial harmony. Having lost an election, the elected representatives of the minority parties continue to participate in the political process so as to influence the actions of the majority party and to improve their position for the next election. If those who have supported the losing party are so dissatisfied as to feel captives in a structure that offers them too little hope, their only alternative may be to leave the system entirely, by 'dropping out' or emigrating.

Some important features of this kind of situation can be highlighted by employing the terminology introduced by Alfred O. Hirschmann in his 1970 book *Exit, Voice, and Loyalty*. People belong, in one way or another, to a variety of organizations; they belong because, in their eyes, the benefits they draw from membership in the present and anticipated future exceed the costs of membership. If it becomes no longer worth maintaining their membership they leave: this is the 'exit' solution. Sometimes, however, exit is impossible, or the costs of exit are disproportionately high, and then people are locked into groups, as Protestants and Catholics in Northern Ireland are constrained by the structure of their society. When exit is out of the question, dissatisfied members are obliged to campaign to change the policies of their group so as to secure greater benefits: this is the 'voice' solution. Benefits and costs are assessed in a way that includes emotional rewards and punishments as well as material ones. Someone who has identified himself or herself emotionally with a particular group or party over a long period cannot easily disconnect. One characteristic of loyalty is that people may continue to care about the progress of an organization even after they have left it.

An executive body may be able to enforce a 'no discrimination' policy or one of 'affirmative action' when it controls the relevant resources and the exit costs are high, as, for example, the United States federal government could prohibit the award of contracts to companies unable to comply with fair employment practices criteria. It is much more difficult to enforce a policy that depends upon the cooperation of constituent members, especially if their exit costs are low. Some bodies (and the Trades Union Congress is a possible example) adopt policy declarations pledging themselves to combat racial discrimination but lack the resources or opportunity to establish any effective methods for enforcing them.

When examining behaviour as an outcome of individual calculations about relative cost and benefit, it is essential to note the ways in which these costs and benefits are themselves influenced by institutional structures. It is easier to get some kinds of policy adopted and easier to get some kinds implemented. The task of formulating and implementing a policy to promote racial harmony in Britain was a novel one. No previous policy problem had presented the same features but as good a one as any with which to compare it was that of reducing atmospheric pollution. The next few paragraphs summarize Roy Parker's account (Hall *et al.*, 1975: 371–409) of 'the struggle for clean air' in order to draw attention to some of the special features of the struggle for racial harmony.

Atmospheric pollution in Britain was a consequence of the great increase in the burning of coal in the nineteenth century for generating industrial power and warming houses, but its deleterious effects were left almost untouched by the sanitary reforms of that era. The Public Health Act of 1936 defined the emission of smoke in any manufacturing process, or from other than domestic chimneys, as a 'nuisance'. Those responsible could be taken to court; but the maximum penalty was only £50, there were many obstacles to enforcement and domestic chimneys (which emitted nearly half of all the smoke in the air) were unaffected by the act. The authorities recognized that there was a problem but declined to accord it a high priority. In 1946, for example, the Simon Committee declared that 'we cannot afford to depress and destroy the life of our cities by smoke pollution', but top priority after the Second World War was given to the alleviation of the housing shortage. Possible measures to introduce new kinds of domestic stoves and to increase the supply of smokeless fuel were neglected; unless the central government took an active lead in dealing with these and other problems, the local authorities could achieve little. The need for action was explained from time to time by a pressure group, the National Smoke Abatement Society, which had a history going back to 1899 and which presented evidence to a series of official committees of enquiry. Its successes were few. No political party could be persuaded to make pollution control a part of its programme, perhaps because there seemed to be no votes in it. The public appeared resigned to the nuisance; they liked their open fires and would have reacted against proposals for legislation restricting their liberty and requiring them to change their habits. Effective controls could have been expensive for manufacturers and domestic users. Central government officials were conscious of the obstacles, inclined to leave the problem to the local authorities, and easily fell back upon the maxim: 'when in doubt, do nothing'.

Public awareness of the seriousness of the problem was blunted because its impact was so diffuse. If an elderly person suffering from chronic bronchitis died during a fog, the polluted atmosphere was seen as advancing only slightly the death of someone whose days were numbered in any case. It took time before all the various returns were received and the number of such deaths could be ascertained. Nevertheless, the gravity of the problem could be appreciated by anyone who studied the evidence. The combination of pollution and a naturally occurring fog resulted in what was called a 'smog'. In 1948 a five-day London smog resulted in somewhere between 700 and 800 more deaths than would otherwise have been expected. Another in 1952 was responsible for at least 4,000 extra deaths. On both occasions the newspapers commented upon the inconvenience to the 'travelling public' but found no news value in the threat to health. After the 1952 disaster some questions were asked in parliament. The London County Council and the National Smoke Abatement Society pressed for action. Yet for a time it seemed as if the scale of the emergency and the ever-present threat of recurrence were insufficient to compel the Minister of Housing and Local Government to take the initiative in respect of a matter which was not one of his department's priorities. The following year, however, he appointed another committee of enquiry, this time under the chairmanship of an industrialist, Sir Hugh Beaver.

In 1954 the committee recommended that the pollution rising from the domestic chimney simply had to be brought under control. Local authorities should have powers to establish both smokeless zones and smoke control areas. Financial assistance should be available for the conversion of domestic appliances. Proposals for reducing industrial smoke were included. The report was sympathetically received by the press and the prospects of action were improved by the appointment of a minister less concerned to build houses and more sensitive to consider-ations of amenity. At this point several Members of Parliament pressed for implementation of the report. A private member's bill was intro-duced, and then taken over by the government with a promise to bring in comprehensive legislation. This did not mean that battle had been won. A general election seemed likely. The Conservatives were far from confident that they would be returned and thought this the kind of measure best introduced by a new government less anxious about deadlines or political popularity. These fears proved unjustified, for a bill was introduced which, early in 1956, became the Clean Air Act.

In discussing the circumstances which contributed to this outcome Roy Parker attributes significance to the 'harassing barrage' of pressure kept up by some twenty Members of Parliament, from both sides of the house, over nearly two years. Industrial smoke pollution was also a sign of wasteful (and therefore expensive) fuel consumption; so it was appropriate for the government to offer industry loans and tax incentives to install more efficient equipment. The growth of motor transport might add to the pollution problem. Yet technological changes could also be cited as a reason for government inaction. The railways were changing from steam power to electricity and diesel fuel. In the Potteries gas and electric kilns were coming into use. The adequate supply of smokeless fuel remained uncertain, while the desirability of economizing in the use of existing fuels might of itself lead to the adoption of better modes of utilization. However, once the act was on the Statute Book, the problems became unacceptable; for after a slow start the local authorities deployed their new powers. By 1971 the weight of smoke discharged into the atmosphere had fallen to 65 per cent of the 1954 figure. In 1970 it was said that for an outlay of three shillings per head per annum the duration of sunshine in London during the months November to January had been increased by about 50 per cent.

The struggle for clean air offers a useful parallel against which to assess the difficulties of getting parliament to adopt legislation against racial discrimination and the problems of implementing policy. It is a useful parallel in another sense too. Clean air and racial harmony are both in the general interest, although it is a matter of subjective judgement whether any particular proposal is, on balance, worthy of support. Economists would describe both clean air and racial harmony as 'public goods' and oppose them to atmospheric pollution and racial friction as public bads. If clean air, like clean water to swim in, were something an individual could purchase for his own use, then, in the economists' terminology, it could be a private good. There cannot be private ownership of the air people breathe: if it is clean for one person it is clean for everyone in the vicinity, which is why it is a useful example of what is meant by a public good. Atmospheric pollution occurs because the sanctions upon individuals or companies who discharge noxious gases are insufficient to discourage them. The pollution gives rise to a public cost. When the sanctions are ineffective the pollutor can treat his reduction of the public welfare as a consideration external to his private operations. The public cost does not feature in his account, but when the sanctions are increased he has to compare the costs which would arise from legal action against him with the costs of installing and operating equipment for purifying the discharge: this makes pollution a consideration internal to his private operations. Racial discrimination resembles pollution in that when the sanctions against it are weak, a discriminator can behave antisocially. Without being penalized, he can increase a social problem which imposes costs both upon the victim group and upon society as a whole, most obviously in the form of race riots.

Just as people who live close to a source of pollution have greater interest in remedial action than people who live far away, so members of racial minorities have a greater interest in the reduction of racial discrimination than members of the majority. They are more likely to commit themselves to work for inter-racial organizations because they hope in this way to benefit present and future members of their minorities. The greater chances of their experiencing discrimination in the organizations which they might otherwise join may also be a contributory factor at this unconscious level. Commitment to work for an organization can be seen as an investment of emotional and other resources in return for the psychological or material benefits that are expected to arise at some stage. Of course, an investment that seems worthwhile to one person may not appear worthwhile to someone with a different set of preferences.

Members of the majority may favour racial harmony as they favour clean air and a long list of other good causes, but they are less likely to perceive the general interest as being important to them individually. Whereas actions to reduce racial discrimination are unlikely to entail costs for minority members they may well do so for majority members since it is they who have to change their ways to reduce the incidence of discrimination. Some majority members will set psychological value upon arrangements which allow them to associate with people with whom they can identify, including here people of similar physical appearance as well as people of similar social background, opinions, and socio-economic status. Whether such a disposition is morally justifiable is another matter, but changes from customary patterns of association do impose psychological costs upon the people who have to make the adjustment.

The general interest has to be promoted by the political process. As the clean air example may have suggested, this depends for its effectiveness upon the realization by interest groups (of whatever size) that they have an interest in common; upon their being able to formulate a practical programme; and upon their winning support for their proposals. In very many cases further progress then depends upon the introduction of legislation followed by effective action to implement the policy. The process is speeded up if interests are represented by agencies able to bargain about priorities by promising support on other issues provided their special claims receive attention. It is easier to carry a proposal through to the point of legislation if in the first place there is reliable information indicating that the benefits to be expected outweigh the costs entailed, and, in the second place, if it features in an order of priority to which a party or institution is committed. Since members of such bodies have a right of exit, commitment depends upon this being too unattractive an option for many to choose it. To obtain commitment a party or institution must also be able to deal with the free-rider problem, for, as has been explained, people do not give of their own resources to try to attain a public good unless they think it worthwhile, that is, unless the amount of the public good they obtain, plus any private benefit they may get (e.g. some people enjoy being leaders) is greater than the private cost they incur. For this reason it is difficult, by purely voluntary measures, to organize action to create or extend a public good. Activists therefore try to work through existing institutions in order to get the government to pass laws which will achieve by legislation what they cannot achieve by general agreement, and, since members of the public appreciate that this is often the only way to achieve a desirable result, they do not usually object when such measures become law. Thus legislation against racial discrimination is like self-commitment in favour of a closed shop. In the sense in which economists use the expression, a public good is one available to all members of a group. The reduction of racial discrimination is a public good for members of racial minorities because it benefits them. To be accounted a public good it does not have to bring a net benefit to members of the majority as well, though in this case the reduction of racial friction is clearly in the public interest also. Interaction between majority and minority members which results in greater racial harmony can be seen as a positive-sum game in which everyone benefits. The big question is whether, in the circumstances of modern Britain, that outcome could be better attained by the appearance of racial minority political agencies, able to bargain on behalf of their minorities by delivering votes to the political parties in return for their promises to implement particular measures, or whether it could be better promoted by majority members coming to believe that it is in their interest to accord a high priority to proposals which will reduce the likelihood of friction and resentment.

3

The end of empire

One of the commonplaces of inter-group relations is that conflict is minimized when members of different groups combine in pursuit of a common objective. This principle is illustrated by black–white relations in Britain during the Second World War. Commonwealth countries joined Britain in declaring war on Germany, Italy, and then Japan. Seven thousand West Indians were recruited to the Royal Air Force and served in Britain, mainly as ground crews in British bases. A contingent of 345 West Indian technicians was brought to work in munitions factories in the Liverpool region. Some 1,200 men from British Honduras were employed in forestry work in Scotland. After the United States entered the war in 1941, black US military personnel served in Britain. Overseas, the Indian Army was engaged in fighting Britain's enemies in the Far and Middle East. There were incidents of racial discrimination in Britain and the British government was disinclined to stand up to United States personnel who thought that the conventions of the Deep South could be exported to Britain, but the over-riding attitude was that Hitler had to be beaten: everyone who could help attain that objective was an ally, and all other considerations had to be subordinated to this supreme priority.

Once the war was over those sentiments of cooperation lost their power. People's attention shifted to more immediate objectives. A significant proportion of West Indian servicemen and forestry workers either remained in Britain or, after visiting their home countries, came back to look for work. At the same time there was a trickle of immigration from West Africa, mainly of seamen and stowaways. Up to 1948 their numbers were too small to arouse much concern and the issue was seen as primarily a matter of Commonwealth policy; problems relating to the welfare of West Indians and Africans in Britain were handled by a small department in the Colonial Office.

This chapter reviews the response of the British government to post-war immigration from New Commonwealth countries. In 1951 the

Colonial Office Welfare Department was closed and for the next fourteen years responsibility for immigrant welfare was left with the local authorities, assisted very little by central government. During the 1950s the British public came to see New Commonwealth immigrants as competitors for scarce resources of housing, employment and welfare services. It began to appear as if the country had on its hands what many people would have described as a 'race problem'. So immigration policy was revised to give priority to domestic interests; then in 1965 the government recognized the need for a national policy with some degree of central direction.

The arrival of the first party of workers from the West Indies in 1948 took Whitehall completely by surprise. Ministers repeated that, as British subjects, West Indians had every right to come and work in Britain and that, while there, they should receive the same protection from the law as anyone else. The Colonial Office opened new files entitled 'West Indian Migrant Workers in England'. The choice of this title seems in retrospect to reveal an unwillingness to accept that most of the newcomers were likely to be settlers rather than temporary residents, but at the time the choice was not unreasonable since many West Indian workers had previously returned to their homelands after working overseas in North and Central America. It took about ten years before the government acknowledged that a substantial process of settlement was under way and a further eight years for them to agree that if the ideal of equality before the law was to be a reality official policy had to acknowledge the implications of the physical distinctiveness of the newcomers.

Britain had just fought a war that had, in part, been caused by Nazi doctrines of racial inferiority and superiority. Though many white people regarded Negroes as a backward race unlikely, if ever, to catch up with whites, at least they knew that the Nazi view of the race problem was wrong. To most people in Britain at this time black people were still fairly exotic creatures known from books, from Hollywood films, from war-time encounters and from the stories of men who had been to Africa or India. A dark-skinned person could not be sure what sort of reception he or she would get from British people encountered for the first time: it might be embarrassingly friendly; it might be hostile; much depended on perceptions of social status.

Another commonplace in the discussion of racial relations is the contrast between the pattern described for the Deep South of the United States and that for Northeastern Brazil. The United States mode assumes that everyone is either black or white; the Brazilian that people are strung out along a continuous scale of differentiation. Those brought up in the United States have assumed that their kind of classification is the natural one and the Brazilian deviant, though it makes better sense to assume that when peoples interact they will distinguish themselves on several dimensions. This way of doing things was rejected in the Deep South because in the era of slavery whites monopolized the avenues of economic opportunity and distorted the normal processes by which people sort themselves out.

The contrast is best seen in terms of the way one person appraises another when they meet. The logic of the first, or Brazilian, mode of appraisal is that the first party assesses the other's claims to deference on a number of dimensions, such as wealth, education, occupation, costume and physical appearance, giving points for each and adding them up to ascertain the sum total. In such a society there are no racial categories; it is individuals who are ranked. The logic of the second, or United States, mode is that everyone is assigned to one of two categories and that any visible degree of black ancestry places a person in the black category. Someone who scores many points for wealth, education and occupation establishes a claim to relative standing within a category, but no number of points, high or low, can counteract the criterion of physical appearance in assigning a person to a racial category. The first mode of appraisal is the more complex because if it is to be systematic the rules for the scoring of points must be ascertainable. It must be possible to discover the number of dimensions on which claims to deference are accumulated, and the weighting given to each dimension relative to the others. Sometimes wealth is more important than education; sometimes skin colour counts for little by comparison with occupation. Yet so long as a low score for colour can be counterbalanced by high scores on other criteria, the society in question can be said to employ the first mode.

Britain after 1945 was such a society. White people were well aware that some of the coloured people they could see about town in London and the university cities were of great importance in their home countries and that their goodwill was of value to Britain and to the maintenance of the Commonwealth. The riches of Indian maharajahs were legendary. Three Indians had been Members of Parliament. Indians and West Indians had gained fame as cricketers. The Aga Khan, the Indian princes, the African obas, emirs and kings could move about the country without exposing themselves to racial discrimination. Many white people would not have doubted that there were quite a few coloured people in London of distinctly higher status than themselves. There was a continuous scale of status, one component of which was skin colour; the weighting attached to colour was quite high for many relationships, especially marriage, and could at times oppose 'whites' to 'coloured', but it was not an either/or mode of assignment like that across the Atlantic. African seamen in the dockland areas were at the bottom of the social pile not just because of their colour but because they could not command claims to deference on other criteria that would counteract the disparagement of their colour. Shades of complexion did matter, but they were part of a more comprehensive calculation of social status.

Competition for status was a major motivating force throughout British society, as indeed it is in most human societies. Studies of life on housing estates at this time recorded how people at one end defined themselves as 'respectable' and others in another part of the estate as 'rough'. The men were conscious of their standing with their peers at work and in all-male leisure groups, but the home was the domain of the women who were anxious to maintain a respectable front in all possible circumstances. To succeed in this a household had to make optimum use of its income, and so the women sought to keep in check their men's inclinations towards drink and gambling. Bernice Martin (1981: 62) has described the ritual features of traditional working-class life and the way they marked off the front of the house from the back, the activities suited to the different days of the week, the festivals of the year, and so on, as part of a culture of control which was the foundation of such dignity and independence as the people were able to wrest from their environment. It was a culture which left room for newcomers provided they accepted the criteria of respectability on which it was based. The newcomers could be Irish Catholics or black West Indians. Their Catholicism and their blackness would cost them several points; they had to understand why this was so even if they disagreed with it. As strangers they would be an unknown quantity and would have to enter the system at or near the bottom, gradually working their way up as they proved themselves more respectable than others.

Most of these traditional working-class communities have been dissolved by the demolition of the rows of back-to-back terraces and the migration of the people to high-rise blocks and suburban semis. It has been a process of assimilation in the older sense of that word, that which denotes an increase in similarity. The impulses underlying this process have been technological: the motor car, the telephone, the computer and a host of other machines require their users to behave in a standardized manner and supersede the customary ways at which people acquire dignity in the eyes of their peers. The media of mass communications have reduced many of the regional variations of speech, custom and diet. Almost everyone is exposed to the advertising techniques of the consumer society which persuade them to want things for which previously they have felt no need. Since the word assimilation has become, for some people, a counter in a debating game about the best pattern of majority–minority relations, it is well to emphasize at the outset that one sense in which it has been used is to designate a process of cultural change that can apply to any group. Since minority members and majority members alike are subject to similar influences deriving from technological change, it is to be expected that some cultural differences between them will diminish. Since minority members are, by definition, in a weaker position, it is also to be expected that at least some of them in some circumstances will seek to conform to majority ideas of what constitutes respectability.

At the beginning of this chapter it was suggested that, after 1945, British people – or at least the educated public – perceived that relations between whites and non-whites gave rise to problems that rarely arose in relations between whites and whites. What kind of explanation could be advanced to take the place of pre-war conceptions of the race problem? In the 1980s two general kinds of answer are current. The first states that differences of skin colour, hair form, facial appearance, etc. (i.e. those differences which are popularly defined as racial) are used as signs in the calculation of an individual's entitlement to deference in a scale of social status, and, where such categories exist, signs indicating to which racial category they should be assigned. The second states that the idea that individuals naturally belong in racial categories is a product of a capitalist social order which favours the dissemination of ideologies which will support that order. The first answer appeals more to people who have adopted a liberal political philosophy; the second to those who favour a radical one. In so far as a conservative answer can be delineated, it tends to resemble the doctrine of the nation expounded by Bagehot and Powell. Since the relative popularity of these three views has affected the way majority–minority relations in Britain have developed, it may be convenient to describe them in the course of a chronological account of the formulation of official policies concerned with those relations.

First of all it is advisable to emphasize that political attitudes do not fall into neat patterns, and the use of the adjectives conservative, liberal and radical as labels for general views of racial relations should not be taken as implying that someone holding such a view votes for any particular political party. There may be a statistical probability that someone who votes Conservative will subscribe to what is here described as a conservative view of the nature of group boundaries, a conservative view of immigration requirements, a conservative view of what is currently called multi-cultural education, a conservative view of how housing or employment policy may best counteract racial disadvantage, and so on, but some Conservatives have been liberals on immigration, some Liberals are radicals in respect of education, and some who consider themselves left-wing Socialists take a decidedly nationalistic view in arguing that white people should be at the head of the queue for scarce resources. There is value in differentiating conservative, liberal and radical positions, but care should be taken in applying these labels.

In the 1950s the main debate was between the conservatives and the liberals. The conservatives were inclined to see both the biological and the cultural differences as very ancient and as important to the maintenance of the identity of the political units with which people identified. These differences could well serve functions which the present generation did not fully understand. The conservative outlook claimed to accept the world as it was, acknowledging present ignorance in order to stress pragmatic possibilities. It was sceptical of the possibilities of social engineering (and therefore doubtful, for example, about the modification of housing or employment policies to improve the position of minorities or of changing the school curriculum). On immigration, conservatives might well disapprove of the settlement in Britain of coloured immigrants but believe that the absorption of small numbers was a small price to pay in support of the much more important policy of trying to maintain Commonwealth unity.

Whereas the conservatives took prevailing British attitudes as a datum on which to build an appreciation of the policy problems, the liberals were critical of those attitudes as ethnocentric, and as the source of much of the tension. The English, like other peoples, perceived members of other nations as differing from them in a continuous scale, with the distance increasing sharply once physical differences were added to cultural ones. Liberals advanced the then revolutionary argument that attitudes of prejudice were learned and not inherited. If they were learned, they could be modified; people could be brought to see that they shared common interests with members of distant societies and that future peace might depend upon their being loyal to trans-national ideals. Liberals denied that there was any race problem, averring that there was a series of problems calling for a variety of remedies each related to particular circumstances. In social life race acquired significance only as a way in which social and cultural differences were identified. So liberals wanted a colour-blind immigra-tion policy, and an international approach to education, stressing parity of esteem *as individuals* for all children irrespective of their appearance and ethnic background. They believed that resources within the housing, employment and other sectors, were best allocated by market processes but that the rules on which markets operated should be drawn up so as to serve social ends.

The connections between views of immigration and Commonwealth policy were close in the early 1950s. Social surveys in 1951 and 1956 revealed that nearly three-quarters of the British population believed that Britain would be 'worse off' without her colonies. This helps explain why it was that at this time somewhere between 46 and 72 per cent of the population (depending upon the way in which their answers were interpreted) approved of free entry to Britain for colonial workers. Sometime around 1958 attitudes toward New Commonwealth immigra-tion started to change. One reason for this was the weakening of the Commonwealth connection as it became clear that the colonies were set on the road to independence and that Britain's economic future lay in closer association with Europe. Immigration from the West Indies had been most in the news but by this time immigration from India and Pakistan was increasing and, in view of the size of the population in those countries, threatened to become substantial. Working-class whites were increasingly perceiving coloured immigrants as competi-tors for scarce resources, especially housing (which was regarded as one of the underlying causes of the 1958 rioting in Notting Hill). Thus New Commonwealth immigration came to be seen as a domestic problem; political prudence dictated that the influx be reduced and regulated in accordance with national economic policy. So in the same year, 1962, that Britain entered the European Economic Community, legislation restricting Commonwealth immigration came into effect.

Perceptions of immigration must also have affected white attitudes towards coloured people resident in Britain. The author has elsewhere (1983: 103–9) advanced a theory which holds that the importance of racial characteristics lies in the way they are used as signs in the ordering of social relations. How would the changes of the immediate post-war period be interpreted by that theory?

It was claimed earlier that many white people in England would not have doubted that there were coloured people of higher status than themselves. In Britain there was the occasional visiting potentate from India or Africa; there was a sprinkling of black and Asian doctors (such as Hastings Banda, later President of Malawi); there were colonial students (some of whom, like Kwame Nkrumah and Julius Nyerere also became presidents); there were a few black and Asian seamen, industrial workers and pedlars. The English person meeting a black or Asian could not place him socially by skin colour alone. At this time a dark complexion was a sign of overseas, probably colonial, origin. In interpersonal relations it designated the dark-skinned person as a cultural stranger, someone who might not understand the norms governing social relations in Britain. In respect to the calculation of social status, a dark complexion was a single negative attribute that had to be assessed along with a range of other attributes. Had all the dark-skinned people been princes and potentates their colour would have been a sign that the people in question were of high status. Had they all been pedlars their colour would have been taken as a sign of very low status. This use of a statistical association as a sign of what may be expected points to a fundamental feature of social relations that is not limited to relations between people assigned to different races.

Just as white people acquire expectations of what those coloured people whom they encounter are going to be like, so male employers acquire expectations of the characteristics of female employees (or elderly employees or youthful employees). These expectations derive from information acquired personally or at second hand through the remarks of others or through stories in the newspapers. This information is subject to certain kinds of distortion but it does in some measure reflect the distribution of attributes in the group in question. If a lot of the coloured people in a town are of high status, skin colour will be used as a kind of short cut in the calculation of expectations and it will be used as a sign of high status. In the years after the war the dark complexion of a young person in the university cities created the expectation that he or she was a student; the dark complexion of a man in the dockland areas created the expectation that he was or had been a seaman; but the coloured population was so small and diverse that over the country as a whole it could not be used as a statistically reliable indicator of a person's social status.

In the 1950s that started to change. Though some of the West Indian workers were skilled tradesmen, an increasing proportion lacked any such qualification. They came with little capital, lacking the contacts and local knowledge that can be important in competition for the better-paying jobs. Employers hired them only if they could not recruit satisfactory white workers. The immigrants could obtain housing only in the declining inner city areas that were going down in status. The Asian immigrants as they came in reinforced the image of the coloured minorities as suitable for the jobs Englishmen did not want, so that a dark colour became a sign of low social status. After the upturn in unemployment in 1956, some whites were no longer so sure that there were jobs that could safely be handed over to a new under-class. A dark colour came also to be a sign of an illegitimate competitor for scarce resources valued by the native working class. Many Labour voters came to adopt a conservative position on coloured immigration. In its intellectual form, this is the argument that for a group of people to constitute a nation they must have a feeling of identity and continuity with their past. England's past was that of a white nation. For those English people who valued this particular sense of history the attempt to add to the nation a group who manifestly lacked such roots was asking a great deal. Only if such a group was relatively small could it be accepted. Lord Radcliffe, a distinguished judge, spoke for many of them when he defined Britain's problem as that of 'inserting into a fairly complex urban and industrial civilisation a large alien wedge, which is in many ways as ready to isolate itself within that community as some members of the community are to keep it isolated' (1969: 39). He criticized the liberal approach to multi-racialism as having been too intellectual: 'it has been over the heads but below the hearts of many of those who are directly affected'. Talk of Britain as a multi-racial society was premature so long as the meaning of such an expression was undecided. Labour voters attracted to a conservative position on immigration were more likely to present the historical link simply and directly, saying that they and their ancestors had fought for the country and built up the welfare state, so they had first claim upon it. Those who subscribed to the liberal position objected that if arguments of this kind were to be advanced they should be directed towards all immigration, not just that of people with dark complexions. The problem of race was not one that Britain had unnecessarily created by admitting people of a different colour, for as long as there were British people disposed to discriminate, a problem existed irrespective of how many people there were who might suffer as a result of this disposition. The difficulties liberals had in getting others to see that in this respect the size of the minority was irrelevant supports the claim that the racial element in racial tension stems from the way racial characteristics are used as signs or indicators of people's entitlements as these are popularly conceived. It is also compatible with the thesis that capitalist relations encourage such a use of physical characteristics. The development, after 1968, of the radical challenge to the liberal interpretation is discussed in Chapter 6.

These differing political philosophies are associated with contrasting views of the politics of immigration in the 1960s. According to the present author the immigrants came to be perceived as competitors for scarce resources, most notably in housing. In such circumstances attempts to exclude any category of competitors who can be separately identified are to be expected; the readiness with which these competitors could be identified by race made exclusion easier; the heritage of ideas about race reinforced this process but was of a secondary character. According to the other view there would have been no significant level of hostility towards the immigrants had they been white and therefore the hostility was racial in its motivation. It led to a system of immigration control designed to reduce the number of black and Asian settlers irrespective of labour demand. Since competition and race were two dimensions of the same historical evidence there can be no simple method for determining the importance to be attributed to either one in relation to the other.

The growing popular hostility towards New Commonwealth immigration was one factor in the policy equation. (By New Commonwealth countries is meant the former dependent territories of Africa, Asia and the Caribbean as opposed to the dominions, but historically the expression is not altogether accurate since countries like Barbados and Bermuda were British long before Canada and Australia.) The three other main factors were Commonwealth policy, official estimates of labour demand, and perceptions of the social consequences of immigration. They will be discussed only in brief.

It is sometimes argued that the hostility to immigration was a sentiment whipped up for their own purposes by agitators motivated by racial prejudice. On the other hand, it can be maintained that politicians were forced, against their own wishes, to introduce immigration controls because of the strength of opinion among their constituents. Evidence can be adduced in support of both these contentions. Neither of them provides a sufficient explanation of the course of political events at the time.

Government ministers listened to advice from their civil servants. In the mid 1950s several colonies were moving towards independence as equal members of the Commonwealth. The stress on the importance of the multi-racial character of that body meant, according to Nicholas Deakin (Rose, 1969: 209), that the Commonwealth Relations Office, perhaps even more than the Colonial Office, had a vested interest in staving off any measure (like that of restrictions upon entry rights for Commonwealth citizens) which might revive notions of the dependent or separate status of the African or West Indian colonies. At the end of the decade the government was anxious to help in the creation of the West Indian Federation and believed that immigration control might hamper that policy: lobby correspondents were given to understand that control would have to be postponed until the Federation had established itself; that was, until 1962 at the earliest.

How officials assessed labour demand is more difficult to discover. The Colonial Office had established an advisory committee on labour immigration in 1947. Ministers were aware of the number of unfilled work vacancies, especially for skilled workers, but they may also have believed that a labour shortage would create pressure for the increased capital investment and structural reorganization which were in the country's long-term interest. There appears to have been little attempt to assess the long-term social implications of a reliance upon New Commonwealth workers. The focus of attention was upon the immigrant generation with little consideration of how many would settle permanently in Britain or what would happen to their children. Immigration, employment, health, social services and education were the concern of different government departments.

It would seem that by the end of 1954 opinion in Whitehall had swung in favour of immigration control, but any governmental decision was postponed until after the election in May 1955. Then the balance was tipped the other way by the arguments of Commonwealth policy and the hopes of controls to be imposed voluntarily by the sending countries. In the government's list of priorities the Commonwealth objectives ranked above the domestic arguments for control. After the Notting Hill disturbances of 1958 an apparently well-informed commentator in The Economist reported that officials 'think that the liberal line − uncontrolled immigration − can be held for a few more years . . . when the tide of colour rises to a ceiling as yet unspecified . . . British voters will demand that some check is imposed' (Rose, 1969: 214–15). They were not far out. Those demands increased. By 1960 the Home Office favoured control. When, next year, plans for the West Indian Federation collapsed and Mr Iain Macleod left the Colonial Office, the path was clear to bring in a bill.

Nicholas Deakin described the opposition of opinions in the House of Commons as a symbolic conflict: the issue of control was debated by reference to its impact on the Commonwealth. In their attack on the bill the Labour Party's principal spokesman maintained that an expanding economy creates new jobs; the economy could not be run without some immigrant labour; if the country were to experience a recession the numbers of immigrants would quickly fall, resulting in a net outflow. A Conservative who refused to support the bill (Mr Nigel Fisher) contended that two bad arguments had been advanced in its favour. First, the claim that immigration caused 'social strains and stresses' was simply a cover for prejudice; no serious attempt had been made to educate public opinion. Secondly, the allegation that immigration led to unemployment among the native people was without foundation. There were also three good reasons for supporting the bill: that the public wanted control; that there were insufficient houses; and that immigration was increasing steeply, with India and Pakistan able to contribute far more than the West Indies. He judged the bill to be bad for race relations and bad for the Commonwealth. It was an angry debate. No speaker tried to discuss what sort of immigration policy might be in the country's best interest.

In attempting to decide what such a policy might have been, the economic arguments must be of central importance. At the conclusion of a non-technical review of the issues (Rose, 1969: 655) Maurice Peston reported that he was impressed by the greater mobility and flexibility of the immigrant workers; they provided a pool of spare capacity, with propensities to save and to work in the social services sector while imposing a disproportionately small burden on public expenditure. Technological change and industrial reorganization were vital concerns which immigration seemed to have facilitated. In retrospect, of course, this argument loses some of its force. Had it been appreciated that technological change was going to reduce the demand for labour so much, other means of industrial reorganization might have been tried.

Another aspect of the question has come to attention only more recently. While attempts have been made in the twentieth century to increase equality of opportunity, Britain is far from offering the same opportunities to the child of the manual worker and the child of the professional as to the child of the company director. One recent investigation (Atkinson, Maynard and Trinder, 1983) concluded that if a man had been born into a family in which the father was in the bottom 20 per cent for wage income, his chances of being himself in the bottom 20 per cent were 45 out of 100. While the inequality causes dissatisfaction it has not, so far, led to public disorder; it seems as if the level of opportunity is sufficient for the prevailing social and economic order to maintain itself. Yet if to this degree of inequality is added both the extra disadvantage of prejudice evoked by a different appearance, and a set of characteristics by which a disadvantaged minority is identified from one generation to the next, the situation is transformed. The physical identification easily leads to a vicious circle. If it is socially not respectable to have a dark complexion this legitimates discrimination, making upward mobility more difficult and reinforcing the equation of a dark complexion with low status. Such a possibility is the mo:e likely in a country in north-western Europe with a light skinned population than in a Mediterranean country. In the former any degree of darkness in complexion is likely to be taken as a sign of difference in origin, giving rise to an either-or kind of two-category classification. In the latter kind of country while there is a greater range of variation a continuous pattern of grading is more likely.

Any attempt to reach a moral judgement about the position taken up by the contending parties in the 1961-2 debate about immigration should be based upon an appreciation of what could reasonably have been foreseen at the time: yet an attempt to decide who was correct can draw upon a knowledge of what actually happened. Britain already had an immigration policy designed to suit the country's needs, in that non-British applicants for entry had to apply for a work permit. This requirement did not apply to citizens of the Commonwealth who, under the British Nationality Act of 1948, were allowed to enter the United Kingdom freely, to find work, settle, and to bring their families. Australia, Canada and other Commonwealth countries had immigration policies which covered both Commonwealth and non-Commonwealth citizens. Britain was the exception. Britain's use of a relatively non-selective policy for Commonwealth entrants meant that many of the new settlers were people who were obliged to make a massive readjustment in a relatively short period of time. The parliamentary *Home Affairs Committee, 1980-1* report on Racial Disadvantage observed (para. 13):

> change is made more difficult if the migrant does not understand the language of his new country, and is illiterate even in his own tongue. If, added to that, he also has to cope with the change from a rural

> environment to an inner city slum, his problems are manifest. If his wife, by the religious customs of her former home, is used to isolation from other men and their families, her problems are intensified. The great majority of migrants from Pakistan, Bangladesh and even India were in this position . . . No Government has sufficiently thought through the difficulties of adjustment facing these new citizens, still less provided adequate policies to deal with them.

The committee went on to say (para. 32):

> a high proportion of Asian children are still entering primary school, although born and raised in this country, with little or no English . . . some have emerged from the British educational system seriously disadvantaged by their low level of English. This is appalling . . . no one can succeed if they do not speak the language.

If, in 1961, parliament had set out to formulate an immigration policy to accord with the country's economic interest they would surely not knowingly have endorsed one which implied so heavy a burden of mutual adjustment for both parties.

The economics, the sociology, and the politics of the issue pointed in different directions. Immigration occurred in the 1950s because the jobs were vacant but the employers were under no obligation to provide housing for their new workers. The employers (many of whom were local authorities and public services) got the benefits of immigrant labour without having to meet all the costs it entailed. Many of those costs were passed on for later generations (of both majority and minority origin) to bear. The immigrants entered a highly competitive society in which much inequality is transmitted from one generation to another, so their children were at a double disadvantage (first, from being the children of people unable to give them what is euphemistically called a good start in life, and secondly from being physically distinguished; those who were born overseas and were also late entrants to British schools were at a third disadvantage). To give the immigrants and their children equality of opportunity with their native peers would have necessitated giving them many additional social benefits. A morally correct policy towards the immigrants would have been politically impossible because it would have seemed unfair in the eyes of the native population. In retrospect it looks as if it would have been better had the apparatus of control been established in 1956, though the number of work vouchers allowed need not then have been restrictive. Ideally, too, the powers of the 1968 Race Relations Act to penalize racial discrimination might have been introduced ten years earlier in the wake of the disorders in Notting Hill. Had controls been introduced in 1956 they would have been criticized as a reflection of, or concession to, colour prejudice, since they would have been intended to reduce net immigration from the West Indies and South Asia. They could have been defended as being in the long-term interest of the minority as well as the majority, though that defence would not have satisfied those who believed that prejudiced opinions should be overridden. It could also be argued that the world is becoming increasingly interdependent. Children born in Britain in the 1990s will benefit from growing up in a society in which people are of different appearance and which shows a cultural diversity reflecting in small measure the diversity of the world outside. Those benefits might not have been appreciated by English voters in the 1950s but it is the duty of legislators to look ahead. This is a powerful argument, but it would have been useless for a British government to deploy it when introducing immigration controls unless it could do so with sincerity. The record shows that at that time very few people could grasp such considerations and even fewer would give them priority over day-to-day concerns. The author acknowledges that in 1961–2 he believed Hugh Gaitskell's criticism of the Commonwealth Immigrants Bill completely justified; he thought that the increasing immigration of South Asians might occasion greater strain since they were less ready to conform to British ways; like others at the time he saw the problem as being associated with the first generation of settlement. In retrospect it looks as if the racial motivations of those who campaigned for restrictions caused others, like Gaitskell, to see this issue as primarily one of race and the wider issues of population policy were neglected. It is easy to be wise after the event, but better to be so than not to reconsider one's earlier judgements.

The 1962 Commonwealth Immigration Act extended to all Commonwealth citizens the selective policy which already governed the immigration of aliens, though on a separate basis. Commonwealth citizens and aliens could, of course, enter as tourists or visitors, but if there was any question that they came with the intention of settling, entry might be refused unless they had permission to take up employment. A Commonwealth citizen who had the promise of a specific job would seek a category A voucher before immigrating. One who had a recognized skill or qualification that was in short supply in Britain but no specific job offer could obtain a category B voucher. All others had to apply for a category C voucher, priority being given to those who had served the British government in time of war.

The act was not phrased in racial terms but it had the effect of reducing the immigration of black and Asian people because within the general Commonwealth category it was they who provided the settlers. There was a net inflow from Jamaica and Pakistan, and a net outflow from Britain to Australia and Canada. The act did not attempt to control immigration from the Republic of Ireland because of the near impossibility of controlling movement across the border with Northern Ireland. This increased the appearance of racial discrimination. Controversy about the act has continued because people judge it by different criteria. Some put most emphasis upon the economic interest of Britain; others upon their view of British political interests; yet others start from a desire to reduce the inequality of wealth between rich and poor countries. The respect in which commentators have differed most is their willingness to accept the natives' attitudes towards the immigrants as a constraint upon policy. Some have insisted that any restriction upon immigration because of those attitudes was a capitulation to prejudice. Thus the Community Relations Commission construed its remit broadly enough to assert in its 1972–3 report that 'the suggestion that racial prejudice should be tackled by restricting the entry of its victims is as dangerously irrational as trying to tackle mugging by locking up old ladies'.

One of the obstacles to rational discussion of immigration policy has been this sort of polemic which, characteristically, misrepresents the opposing view. The equation of British attitudes towards people of different colour with the state of mind of men who rob old ladies is only mischievous. Those attitudes include a well-documented element of prejudice, but they are far more complicated than that. Another element, as has been explained, is the way that a dark complexion detracts from a person's claims to social status. Above all, the attitudes towards coloured people in Britain have been compounded with attitudes towards immigration; these are based on a hostility towards competitors of all kinds but are more intense towards those who can be outwardly identified as being of different origin. The attitudes in question often appear fluid and unpredictable because they are conditional. The English will accord social acceptance to people of different origin and appearance in some circumstances and not others. In 1951 a visiting anthropologist from the United States was told by a former seaman in Cardiff 'you can have what the Englishman don't want: you can get the room he won't live in; the job he won't take, and the woman he throws out'. Whites in Britain, as in the United States, have never objected to blacks who wait upon them, entertain them or offer only a limited kind of competition. Thus, quite apart from the variability between English people, there is a variation according to the claims the other party is thought to make: how he or she presents himself or herself; is he or she asking for more than seems reasonable? The greater the size of the immigrant minority the greater is the pressure upon majority attitudes. Whether there were few immigrants or many was irrelevant to the nature of white prejudice as an emotional predisposition to hostility, but it was highly relevant to the rational and conditional element in white attitudes. The task of statesmanship in the 1950s and early 1960s was to lay the foundations for racial harmony in the 1990s by encouraging the positive components in English attitudes. There should have been a serious attempt to educate public opinion. Hostility towards immigration should not have been allowed to increase hostility towards people of immigrant origin resident in the country.

A realization of this underlay the often-quoted statement of Mr Roy Hattersley that 'without integration, limitation is inexcusable; without limitation, integration is impossible'. It underlay the 1965 white paper *Immigration from the Commonwealth*. Part I of this document declared that the controls introduced in 1962 were being evaded and needed to be tightened. Part II proposed to discontinue the issue of employment vouchers to unskilled workers and to reduce the quotas for other categories. It proposed that the Home Secretary should have powers to deport at his discretion immigrants whom he considered to have evaded the controls, and that those suspected of evasion could be required to register with the police in the same way as aliens. Part III outlined measures to assist integration into what was described as 'already a multi-racial society' including the creation of a new National Committee for Commonwealth Immigrants to replace the Commonwealth Immigrants Advisory Council set up in 1962. (A report from that council had led to the establishment of a National Committee for Commonwealth Immigrants in 1964 on a relatively modest basis but it had not superseded the Advisory Council). The good name of Britain, so the white paper said, demanded that Commonwealth immigrants 'should be absorbed into our community without friction and with mutual understanding and tolerance'. The publication of this document marked a change in government priorities in three main respects. First, it recognized that public concerns associated with skin colour were to have greater precedence compared to the common status of citizenship. Secondly, in Deakin's words (Rose, 1969: 229) by further restricting immigration, it marked the end of ten years' battle by the Colonial and Commonwealth Offices, dating from their victory of 1955, to keep

Commonwealth interests in the range of those which would be considered when immigration policy was made; thirdly, it was a significant step in the process by which central government assumed greater responsibility in this field.

The white paper got an unenthusiastic reception from the press because so many people found the proposals distasteful even if necessary (Patterson, 1969: 44–8). Despite the sentiments expressed in Part III its tone was overwhelmingly negative and its emphasis upon the need for controls helped feed the very anxieties about immigration that the controls were supposed to allay. Michael and Ann Dummett (1969: 104–10) contend that Part III was compiled in a different section of the government and was incompatible with the proceeding parts since it repudiated the alleged necessity for restricting immigration. This contradiction was later rationalized, they write, by the assertion that an exclusionist immigration policy was essential if the integration of those already admitted was to be facilitated. The critics have said that it was hypocritical to say to an Asian immigrant 'you are a full citizen with equal rights, but your wife and children must wait years before we shall allow them to come and join you'. The Dummetts maintain that far from appeasing the racialists on the one hand and on the other satisfying the anti-racialists and the immigrants, the government policy had the reverse effect from that intended. It encouraged the belief that immigration caused problems and it failed to deal with prejudice. There is justification for both charges but the reinforcement of the negative image of immigration was a short-term effect likely to last for a decade or so, whereas the adverse effects of inaction could have been much greater. The lack of action against prejudice can in some measure be excused by the absence of reliable information about its costs. Prejudice was easily represented as a natural preference for one's own kind. Politicians and members of the public were reluctant to accept that discrimination could be penalized when individuals were allowed to think and say what they wished in private. How frequently racial discrimination occurred, in what circumstances and with what consequences, no one knew for sure. If good information could be assembled which supported the critics' suspicions, more comprehensive political action might be possible, but policy has to proceed step by step.

Before the white paper appeared the Commonwealth Immigrants Advisory Council had insisted that Britain was becoming a multi-racial society, but they too had provided no indication of what this meant. Unless something definite follows from the acceptance of a proposition of this kind it must be meaningless. At this time the most common official use of the expression 'multi-racial' was to designate overseas territories, especially some of those in the Commonwealth, which were being given new constitutions in the attempt to foster a national unity: Kenya, Rhodesia (Zimbabwe), Mauritius and Fiji had been among them. Multi-racial seemed to convey a stress upon citizenship and, applied to Britain, it implied that since the immigrants had the same rights as the natives the latter should treat them as equals. In this sense the proposition was more than a statement of fact. Yet a sociologist must find all this over-simple. Brazil, Guyana and Mississippi have multi-racial populations but they are very different kinds of society. It is doubtful if these societies (as opposed to their populations) have a single relevant feature in common. Britain might in 1965 be a multi-racial society in the sense that it included a number of culturally distinctive minorities identified by physical appearance; if several generations later that cultural distinctiveness had disappeared and, as in Brazil, only individuals could be distinguished by their appearance, would that also be a multi-racial society? It was, and is, almost impossible to give any meaning to the proposition that Britain should be a multi-racial society. An easier cause was, and is, to contend that obstacles to free association should be removed so that the form of the society can be decided by its individual members as they pursue their own goals.

Sociologists are often ready to criticize the politicians. They, on the other hand, could reasonably expect the sociologists to have clarified the conceptual problems implicit in expressions like assimilation, integration and multi-racial society. In the 1950s and early 1960s, only a handful of sociologists were interested in such topics and they were unable to keep up with the speed at which the political problems developed. For guidance they looked to their colleagues in the United States. Some took over a conception of assimilation which came into use in the United States in the 1910s and 1920s when some writers were perturbed about the quality of immigrants from Eastern and Southern Europe. It was feared that they would not make good Americans and in this way assimilation was equated with Americanization. The confusions in this mode of reasoning were exposed in the United States in the mid 1960s. In Britain the present author (1955: 75, 234–7) represented assimilation as the outcome of a two-way process of adaptation on the part of the minority and acceptance of that of the majority. Most British commentators did not see the need for such distinctions and equated assimilation with Anglicization. Like their American predecessors they assumed that the dominant group absorbs the minority without itself undergoing change; it is a process now sometimes called 'straight line' assimilation, since the minority is thought to conform to the expectations of the majority in all sectors of activity at a uniform speed of change. This conception of assimilation (which was very selective since it usually was not applied to change in religious faith) is one to which minority people not surprisingly object, since it denies any value in what distinguishes their cultures, any possibility of their making a contribution to the life of their new society, or any freedom for them to choose between different alternatives in the process of responding to the pressures upon them. As a way of designating a more desirable outcome of social interaction, the expression 'integration' was at this time preferred because it seemed to make better allowance for the perpetuation of minority distinctiveness in the private realm.

The concepts of assimilation and integration occasion confusion because they are applied both to individuals and to groups. Immigrants adapt to a new society by changing their individual ways; if individuals change in similar fashion people speak of the minority as having changed, or of the majority as having altered so as to adjust to their presence. Sometimes, too, immigrants attempt to translate their shared individual experience into collective action as a means of putting pressure on the majority. This aspect forms the subject of the next chapter.

4

Ethnic mobilization

People may choose to seek their ends either by individual or collective action. For immigrants the choice between these two strategies may be both important and problematic. Collective action in their new country may be a carry-over of common procedures in their old country or it may be based on a perception of common interests in their new one. Yet it is more difficult for them to organize collectively within the receiving society since they stand in different relations to that society and therefore have different interests. Some immigrants have a happier experience of the receiving society and try to conform to what they think that society expects of them. This is usually discussed as evidence of assimilation and that process has a major effect upon the possibility of ethnic mobilization.

The previous chapter criticized the popular misconception of assimilation according to which the majority sees itself as absorbing the minority. It maintained that the processes of cultural change are much more complex and affect members of the majority as well as the minority, but did not go into any detail. Nor did it make explicit the presumption that most cultural change can be understood in terms of the same principles as those which explain changes in consumer behaviour. People have taken to buying plastic kitchenware in place of enamel goods because the plastic gives them what they want more cheaply. Traditional working-class culture has crumbled before the desire for the semi-detached suburban house and the family motor car. Similar pressures bear upon members of ethnic minorities. In line with the bargaining perspective employed in this book, it can be useful to look at the processes of assimilation as resulting from individual calculations of the benefits and costs of different courses of action in a context of changing preferences.

The consumer's preferences for a particular kind of kitchenware or a particular brand of tomato soup are unproblematical from a psychological point of view. Producers try to cultivate 'brand loyalty', but for the most part a consumer can change from one brand to another without finding it an emotional wrench. It is very different with respect to ideas about how a husband and wife should behave towards each other, or parents and children. As individuals grow up they internalize the values of the culture around them; they commit themselves psychologically to notions of what a man and a woman should be like and build up their own personalities accordingly. These are the components of culture that change most slowly, and then change stems mainly from the death of the old generation and its replacement by one which has been differently socialized. Thus in a situation of immigration members of the majority population have an emotional commitment to patterns which obtained before the entry of the newcomers. Members of the minority are tied in a similar way to values embodied in the culture of their homeland. Obviously, members of both the majority and the minority will differ among themselves in their emotional attachments: some features of the society in which they grew up they will value positively, others negatively. The principles are the same for both majority and minority members but, since the pressures upon the latter to change are the greater, it may be simpler to examine them from the immigrant standpoint.

Those features which bind a person to his or her society of origin (the sending society) can be represented as 'pull' factors; those features in the society from which he or she would like to escape are then 'push' factors. The contrary influences attracting an immigrant to his or her new society (the receiving society) can be represented in the same way. The factors vary in their strength. The bigger the cultural gap between the sending society and the receiving society, the bigger the incentive needed to induce someone to change from one pattern to another. Generalizing drastically (in order to explain the nature of the argument rather than provide a proper example of its application in empirical research), it can be said that the bulk of Asian immigrants to Britain have felt a strong pull towards the sending society and its culture: they see their kinsfolk as offering them an emotional and material security they can obtain nowhere else. This culture, though, is also one which entails many close constraints for anyone who would live within it; these constitute a kind of rent that has to be paid by all members of the society and the migrant would sooner avoid having to pay it. The receiving society's attractive features are the opportunities to earn substantial monetary rewards and to minimize traditional constraints, but they are balanced by the repulsive features of English culture such as the disregard for the norms of propriety important in Asian culture, particularly those which, by controlling the sexuality of the women members, protect the honour of the kin group, and those which entitle members of the grandparental generation to a dignified old age.

Asian immigrants came to Britain as sojourners, planning to save money in order to return home, but continually postponing that day so that most became settlers. To start with they were single males, ready to conform externally to English expectations if that helped them obtain good wages. As their wives and daughters joined them so little bits of Punjabi culture were reassembled in British cities. In the Punjab families compete for *izzat*, or prestige, even more fervently than the English compete for status (because, as explained in Chapter 2 the competition is more a contest between groups). Roger and Catherine Ballard (1977: 33), in their description of the development of Sikh settlements in Britain, write that 'That most significant transformation in overseas settlements came about when these too became arenas in which *izzat* could be gained or lost. Once this occurred, all migrants had to compete or else lose face.' The Sikh migrant was then subject to contrary pulls and pushes, not between the sending society and the receiving society, but between the transplanted sending society and the receiving society.

Immigrants from the West Indies felt an emotional pull from their sending societies on account of their socialization and because they appreciated the fellowship of peers who had known the same joys and sorrows. That pull was for them less strong than the corresponding one among Asians because their culture was less complex and the countervailing push of poverty had for some time turned people's minds towards emigration. They were attracted by the monetary rewards available in the receiving society, but their initial readiness to conform to the ways of that society was blunted by the experience of white prejudice evoked by their colour. Not all West Indians were black, of course, and the significance of blackness can be better appreciated by considering the differences in the positions of a white West Indian and a black. Both would be subject to similar pull and push factors from their sending societies. As an incentive to conform to British ways the white West Indian would be offered the prospect of economic and status rewards comparable to those available to a New Zealander, Australian or Irishman of similar skills. The black West Indian could look forward only to competing with a substantial handicap, one that would be transferred to his children who might well be caught in the trap of transmitted deprivation. Some black West Indians found the incentives to stay in Britain sufficient; others emigrated to North America or the Caribbean; yet others have tried to create a distinctive culture in Britain by amplifying those features which make them distinctive.

	Sending Society	Receiving Society
Asians: pull	Emotional and material security	Monetary rewards
push	Social constraints	Impropriety
West Indians: pull	Fellowship of peers	Monetary rewards
push	Poverty	White prejudice

The initial position of Asians and West Indians with respect to processes of assimilation in Britain can be represented in a simplified way in the diagram above. It seeks to represent cultural change as the product of individual response to a variety of positive and negative features, operating with different strengths for different individuals. But it is only a starting point since the initial simplicities are soon complicated by new factors that cannot be represented in such a diagram. Pakistani immigrants in Britain have used their new wealth to seek goals that were beyond their reach before emigration. The institution of *purdah* by which the women are confined has become more restrictive, increasing the culture gap (Dahya, 1981); this is a feature of the attempt to observe religious norms more closely, following a process that has been called Ashrafization (Jeffery, 1976). Sikhs in Britain have been affected by a revivalist movement in the Punjab, West Indians by the elevation of black consciousness originating in the United States. These movements have added new pull factors. To see how they operate it is necessary to focus on one cultural feature at a time, taking, say, the question of what a male wage earner should do with his wages: should he tell his wife what they are? Should they divide them together? Should he give her a fixed sum each week? Should he be free to spend his share as he pleases? Is the answer different if his wife is also a wage earner? If a single feature is examined, it is then possible to study how both majority and minority norms have changed over a period of time; whether they have changed so as to become more or less similar; why they have changed in that direction, and at that speed. Only by examining the detail can the processes be comprehended.

These processes are so complex that the only way to study them is by starting with simple propositions and then introducing qualifications according to whichever aspect of change is of chief interest. Previous paragraphs have implied that, as a first approximation, cultural change on the part of immigrants can usefully be seen as the response of individuals to two sets of incentives, those which reward the individual for conforming to the practices of the sending society and the corresponding pulls from the receiving society. A first set of qualifications have to be added immediately, for individuals do not respond to incentives in a context of isolation. Group membership is not purchased in pennyworths. No individual can decide to have just 73 per cent membership in a group. It often has to be all or nothing. Moreover, the notion of incentives implies that the individual chooses between alternatives offered him from outside whereas group identification is usually something inside the individual's personality as well as outside in the social environment. Nor does that environment necessarily treat the individual as unique. Prejudice is directed against categories rather than individuals so that whatever the individual does, he or she may be unable to escape from other people's stereotypes. A second set of qualifications is no less important. The cultures of both the sending and the receiving societies are changing and are heterogeneous. It may be only a bit of each society that has any influence on a particular individual. Immigrants build up in their new homelands what has earlier been called a transplanted sending society, a modified version of the sending society, which maintains a new intermediate or minority culture; it is this which often contends with the receiving society for the immigrants' conformity.

How the first set of qualifications may operate can be suggested by a study of Jewish identity in north-east London. Interviewers called at houses asking 'are you or any member of this household Jewish?' and in this way established a sample. They found that over 90 per cent of households claimed membership in a synagogue. Since membership fees are substantial they wondered what pragmatic reasons there might be for membership. The most important such reasons, they concluded, were those associated with the ceremonialization of the stages of the life cycle: marriage, reception into adulthood, 'to enrol children in religious education classes and, above all, to receive a Jewish burial'. Being able to attend services in the High Holydays of Yom Kippur and Rosh Hashanah was also important (Kosmin and Levy, 1983: 8). Similar considerations may well motivate people belonging to other minorities distinguished by religious practice and they give rise to what are called 'exit costs'.

Minority members can cease identifying with 'their' minorities and, to the extent to which circumstances permit, may leave these groups. The cost which a London Jew who does this has to bear, is that of doing without synagogue services for life-cycle ceremonies and for worship. These costs may seem unimportant to young people who, if they marry, would be content with a civil ceremony. They may seem much heavier to their parents and heavier yet to the old person whose thoughts turn to his own burial. Thus the pull of group membership may vary from one individual to another and may be related to age, religious belief and other social characteristics.

One of the best opportunities for exploring the influence of push and pull factors is provided by case studies of individuals who experience contrary influences from, on the one hand, the receiving society and, on the other, either the sending society or the minority society. Despite the many books and articles about minority relations there are very few such case studies. One of the best is David Beetham's account of the disputes about the wearing of turbans by Sikh busmen in Wolverhampton and Manchester.

In their homeland in the Punjab, the Sikhs have lately been distinguished not just by their profession of a distinctive faith but by an ethnic movement which, while centred upon the symbols of that faith, presses the Indian government to establish a separate Sikh state. The movement finds political expression in a party called *Sharomani Akali Dal* which has a branch or branches in Britain. Those Sikhs who emigrated to East Africa and Britain found at first that it was easier to obtain employment if they were clean shaven and did not wear turbans. The social structure in East Africa did not discourage communalism and the Sikhs there later came to be conscientious in their turban wearing, a characteristic they brought with them when many moved to Britain after the expulsions of the late 1960s. Sikhs who abandon the turban are described as *patits* or apostates, but at one time it was so widely accepted as necessary to give up the turban in Britain that it was even possible for *patits* to hold positions on the temple management committees. With the immigration of women and dependents, Sikh families were reconstituted in Britain; secularizing tendencies were halted; the best way for a man to achieve status in these transplanted communities was for him to display his faithfulness by observing the symbols of Sikhism. One of these is *kesh*, or unshorn hair, which is supposed to be bound up in a turban. The turban distinguishes the Sikh from members of other Asian minorities, so when Sikh leaders insist that it be worn they make their group more distinctive, cohesive, and reinforce their own leadership positions. There is no symbol or sign of group membership that designates any of the other minorities so clearly as the turban. It brings into sharp focus everything that differentiates the baptized male observer of the Sikh religion. So when a Sikh wearing his turban turned up for work at a municipal bus depot he presented the employer with a clear-cut decision: turbans were either to be permitted or not, for no half-way compromise was possible.

The Wolverhampton dispute started in 1967. At the time the city's transport department employed more than 150 Sikhs, none of whom wore beards or turbans or had advanced any objection to rules against these. One of the Sikh drivers, Mr T. S. Sandhu, was off work for three weeks on account of an illness. He came to believe that his illness was divine retribution for his lapse from the faith, so he determined to let his beard grow and to insist on wearing his turban. When he went back to work he was sent home for failure to observe the regulations. Mr Sandhu then called on the help of Mr C. S. Panchhi, the president of a branch of the *Sharomani Akali Dal* in Birmingham with a few dozen members. Though Mr Panchhi had lived in Britain for ten years he could hardly speak English and communicated through an interpreter. His organization was oriented towards politics in the Punjab and Mr Panchhi subsequently utilized the publicity he obtained from the Wolverhampton dispute when he returned to the Punjab and stood for office there.

Mr Panchhi sought a meeting with the management of the transport department to explain the religious significance of beards and turbans for Sikhs. He failed to come to any agreement, so after two weeks it was declared that Mr Sandhu had dismissed himself by failing to comply with the conditions of employment. The Transport Committee would consider changing those conditions only if requested by the union. So the Sikhs turned out in force for the next meeting of the local branch of the Transport and General Workers' Union. A ballot of the branch was arranged. The West Indian busmen voted with the Sikhs and a motion supporting Sandhu's request was carried 336 to 204. The Transport Committee, however, took no action since they believed that under existing conditions, where all employees were treated alike, there could be no question of discrimination. By this time the dispute was attracting national attention, but the Sikhs, because of the way in which it had been approached, had few allies in Wolverhampton. Bus passengers, when questioned by newsmen, expressed no objection to beard or turban: they were more concerned that the buses should run on time.

The Akali Party proposed to hold a protest march. The leaders of the local Sikh temple thought this might be counterproductive; they preferred to hold a public meeting and to seek cooperation from councillors and Members of Parliament. Their views did not prevail. A march was held; according to one estimate it was supported by 5,000 to 6,000 people. It dramatized the issue as a confrontation in which the Sikhs were seen as attempting to exert pressure by weight of numbers alone. Mr Panchhi next organized a march in London, which was unsuccessful. Leadership of the agitation in Wolverhampton then passed to someone else. Mr Jolly of Hounslow was elected president of the Akali Party in place of Mr Panchhi. He had connections with a different group of politicians in the Punjab. He was acting, he said, on behalf of the '90 per cent of Sikhs' who did not wear the turban and whom he wished to bring back to their faith. He proposed to burn himself alive at the Sikh New Year if no settlement had been reached by then. Having committed himself publicly, any failure on Jolly's part to fulfil his promise would have been considered a disgrace to his religion as well as to his person: he had to go through with it. Both Sikhs and English people in Wolverhampton were incensed by Jolly's action. The government became involved, and there were protest marches in New Delhi. The Wolverhampton Transport Committee then decided to comply with the union's request for the modification of the regulations. Mr Jolly replied, 'This is not my victory, but a victory for all Sikhs.' The secretary of the Sikh temple in Wolverhampton, knowing the damage that had been done to community relations in the town, thought it had not been worth it.

The Wolverhampton dispute can be seen, in the language of game theory, as either a zero-sum or a negative-sum game. Earlier it was said that in India struggles over the relative precedence of sub-castes were zero-sum games. If one group goes up the league table, others must come down by a like amount. This was the kind of orientation that Mr Panchhi and Mr Jolly brought to the affair. A victory for the Sikhs became a defeat for the English. To judge from David Beetham's account the damage to community relations was such that the negative side of the account outweighed the positive. From a sociological standpoint, however, it is interesting that individuals should have been able to exploit such a dispute for their own ends, individuals, moreover, from outside the town; and that once they defined the issue in a particular way it should have been almost impossible to halt a process of polarization. It would seem that most Sikh busmen did not feel as Sandhu did. Maybe they wished the roles changed so that he could wear a beard and turban, but did they wish to do likewise? Did they wish to contribute to a situation in which they would be under greater pressure to conform to the requirements of their religion and get drawn into temple affairs? In view of their previous behaviour it seems improbable. Many of the Sikhs who supported Sandhu's position also wished to solicit support among the English population and to press their claim in a way that did not arouse antagonism. Why then did they go along with actions contrary to their own preferences? It is not easy to offer a simple reply. Part of any answer must be their socialization to particular values and the importance to them of the approval of their peers. Many English people who are not Christians are disinclined to take any public stand against features of that religion (like, say, Sunday observance). When guessing the chances that one's peers may disapprove of one's action, there is a general tendency to play safe and to over-estimate the risk. In most circumstances in which such decisions have to be taken one possible consequence has to be balanced against others, but in the turban dispute it was possible for the activists to isolate this one claim as a priority which, because it touched a man's chances of salvation, could not be put into the scales and weighed against worldly considerations.

In Chapter 2, when discussing bargaining relations, reference was made to the advantage one party can obtain by the skilful use of commitment tactics. If the first bargainer could persuade the other party that he could not possibly settle for anything less than a particular outcome this would reduce the range within which a solution could be found. Mr Jolly's threat of suicide was just such a commitment. The Wolverhampton politicians were unaccustomed to dealing with this kind of threat and regarded it as a kind of blackmail. Mr Jolly's commitment also put pressure on other Sikhs to support his gesture. It was difficult for those who deplored his action to speak publicly against it without seeming disloyal to Sikhism. They became the captives of a group sentiment engineered by an extremist.

The Manchester turban dispute started earlier, in 1959. Mr G. S. S. Sagar applied to the transport department, wearing a beard and turban, for employment as a conductor. He was told that since his turban did not meet the official conditions of service he could be offered work only in the garage. Mr Sagar asked his local councillor to take up his case and this led to a debate in the city council, terminating in a vote by forty-one to thirty-one to maintain existing practice. The next day a local paper published a letter from a group of Sikhs urging him not to press the matter further: 'If they don't like us for particular jobs with our turbans, the letter said, 'we must try to obey them and prove ourselves good citizens.' Mr Sagar disagreed. He continued to lobby for support among both Sikhs and English people, and persuaded the leaders of one of the temples to apply for reconsideration of the issue. The Transport Committee were worried by claims of discrimination and adopted a resolution that they approved of 'the employment of men of any religious belief whatsoever as platform staff, provided they comply with departmental conditions' but this did not satisfy the claimants (incidentally the committee were able to point out that they did employ a Sikh who complied with those conditions, and that he was Sagar's brother). There was then a vote of the city council which upheld their committee's position by sixty-three to forty-two votes.

Officials in the Manchester and Wolverhampton transport departments saw themselves as running a non-political public service; they thought they should be allowed to do this in the most efficient way; conditions of service had to be standard for people of all religions. Union officers regarded the actions of the Sikhs as a challenge to their authority, for it was their function to initiate changes in the rules and they could not allow a question concerning conditions of service to pass out of their hands. The busmen themselves were less worried about it. Since many of them did not wear the caps which were the cause of the dispute, a local ratepayer started a campaign not to pay fares to conductors who were not wearing their caps; and that did arouse the busmen's resentment. Straw polls conducted by newspaper reporters indicated that about eight of ten members of the public disagreed with the ban on turbans but a minority saw the Sikh attitude as evidence of the Sikhs' unwillingness to conform to public expectations in the country in which they wished to settle. To these people the busmen's cap became a symbol of the British way of life that was being disturbed. Comment in the press usually represented the ban as narrow-minded; commentators thought it silly to regard the transport departments' uniform as so special when the Queen had no objection to Sikhs wearing a turban with her uniform. Councillors were disturbed by charges of racial or religious discrimination and perturbed to receive press clippings from as far away as Australia and the United States showing the matter to be of international interest. In such circumstances the leadership of a few influential councillors, in persuading their colleagues to treat the matter as one crossing party lines to be settled with a egard for the city's reputation, made a difference. Thus in 1966 the council voted for a third time, seventy-one to twenty-three, to allow the turban and, after a final hiccup from the Transport Committee, the dispute was over. Mr Sagar declared 'This is a victory for the people of Manchester.' In the language of game theory it can be seen as a positive-sum game in that the Sikhs won something without anyone else losing. Both the council and the Sikhs learned that the existing institutions could be used to settle such disagreements and to do so amicably; community relations were improved. Against this view of the matter it can be remarked that in Manchester it took seven years to get the ban lifted as opposed to nineteen months in Wolverhampton, but then it should also be remembered that the Wolverhampton dispute started eight years later, after other councils had decided to permit turbans to be worn as part of uniforms.

David Beetham (1970: 76–8) describes the contrast between events in Manchester and Wolverhampton as representing two different models of interaction: integrative and alienating (though the second model is also called polarizing). In the first, Manchester model, the dispute helps integrate the minority by increasing the majority's understanding of its expectations (and vice versa), by establishing new contacts, and by developing the existing procedures so as to resolve a new kind of grievance. In the second model, initial failure to obtain support encourages a more militant approach from the minority. Lacking allies and advisers, the minority is more likely to utilize the sort of tactics which increase majority antagonism. It tries to impose a solution by duress and the gulf gets wider. In other circumstances the use of polarizing tactics may not be accidental. A would-be minority leader trying to mobilize his group may act so as to invoke threats from the majority knowing that this will oblige his fellow minority members to come together in self-defence. He will increase the cohesion of his group by exploiting the possibility of aggression from a group to which they stand in a relation of opposition. There was an exchange of threats in the turban disputes. Activists like Panchhi and Jolly were able to persuade Sikhs that their religion was under threat from the English. The attention paid to their protests then suggested that they could severely damage the reputations of the two cities. Disputes involving sections of the native population do not follow such a course because a local politician bargains for a range of services: if he cannot get a new school building for his locality he may be content to obtain a new pedestrian crossing. Minorities which are only partially integrated into the majority society may not be bargaining for a series of objectives but have just one overriding priority. As Nathan Glazer (1975: 211–12) has observed, 'A small group for which one issue is everything may overcome a large group for which the issue is only one among many.' Yet a small group which repeats this tactic runs the same danger as the shepherd boy who cried 'Wolf!' too often.

The turban disputes in Wolverhampton and Manchester have been discussed as illustrations of the first set of qualifications to the proposition that cultural change in a situation of immigration can usefully be seen as the product of two sets of incentives to conforming behaviour. They show, with respect to a single ethnic group, that norms deriving from the homeland culture can be used by that group to mobilize and extract concessions from the majority. They illustrate two different strategies for obtaining such concessions. Yet they are far from representative of the options available to members of ethnic minorities in Britain who wish to pursue shared objectives by bargaining. The Sikhs bring with them to Britain a social and cultural heritage that fosters a distinctive identity and helps the minority organize in ways to which the majority cannot take strong exception. There are very few other examples of ethnic collective action in Britain to compare with the turban disputes. Muslim groups from Pakistan and Bangladesh have competed with one another in the construction of mosques. For one group to build a bigger mosque than another's and get planning permission for a minaret two feet taller is a coup in a zero-sum contest of the kind in which they might engage in their homelands, but some have also organized to persuade the education authorities to pay more regard to their ideas of propriety concerning girls (such as costume for physical education and swimming lessons). Asian groups have utilized the ties of kinship, neighbourhood and ethnic community in industrial disputes when textile workers have taken strike action (often with little support from British trade unions). These activities have usually been directed to the goals of their homeland culture or to goals (like higher wages) which are recognized in both the sending and receiving societies. The Jews have used their ethnic organization in positive-sum bargaining to make it easier for members of any minority to maintain culturally distinctive features which are important to their shared lives. Asians may in due course follow this lead; certainly in Birmingham Sikh and Hindu congregations contributed to the fund-raising campaign of a Punjabi Christian clergyman who set out, with his congregation, to establish a separate church. Yet outside the religious sphere there has been little ethnic collective action by Asians and even less by the ethnic minorities of West Indian origin. This tends to support the claim discussed on pp. 19–22 that the conditions for ethnic mobilization are rarely found, and that when they are it is often as a by-product of some other form of association, such as those deriving from kinship and a common religion.

Ethnic collective action by the minorities of West Indian origin suddenly appeared a possibility in the mid 1960s when the black consciousness movement spread from the United States to Britain. The main effect was to encourage feelings of black pride. West Indians had previously called themselves, and been called, coloured people, an expression used to categorize all non-whites. In the West Indies shades of skin colour were associated with social status, a pale complexion being an occasion for pride. These assumptions, together with the evident colour prejudice of white people in Britain, made many dark-skinned West Indians ashamed of their colour, so that it required a major emotional effort for them to re-evaluate feelings they had previously repressed and to re-define themselves as black. Having done so, this, as in the United States, became a source of emotional strength. The black consciousness movement in the United States drew attention to long-neglected grievances and forced through major political changes. It gave black people in Britain a feeling that, if they were to learn from the experience of the United States, they might be able significantly to improve their position. It also had a potent effect on white opinion, increasing sympathy for the black person as a victim and causing whites to take a more serious view of the political and moral dangers generated by racial inequality. In the United States 'black' was used to designate Afro-Americans and did not include brown-skinned Hispanic-Americans (like Puerto Ricans and Mexican-Americans) or native Americans (more commonly referred to as Indians). Since in Britain 'coloured people' was a designation for all non-whites some people thought it logical to use black as a substitute in an equally inclusive sense. This was done first in 1965 when a leaflet publicizing the Racial Action Adjustment Society was prepared by a black visitor from the United States, and then in 1968 given academic endorsement by Professor Michael Dummett in an address to a conference arranged by the Institute of Race Relations. Its usage could be justified by the argument that it was whites who had marked off non-white people as a separate category to whom they accorded fewer privileges and therefore all those so excluded needed to combine to overcome white prejudice. In practical terms it aimed to create a maximal constituency. In the United States

Afro-Americans were numerous enough to organize as a political minority. In Britain, Afro-Caribbeans were a tiny unit. Calling all non-whites black was an attempt to combine all the various coloured minorities into a unit big enough to bargain with the whites. It was a tactic that polarized relations on the assumption that this was the best way to get rid of white prejudice. It was a usage that appealed to black and white activists of a radical persuasion because it harmonized with their view of society (as discussed in Chapters 3 and 6) but, given the very different orientation of nearly all members of the various Asian minorities, not to speak of the tensions between people of African origin over against the Caribbeans, and of differences between Caribbeans, it was improbable that the rhetoric could ever be translated into a genuine political organization; in this respect it may have fostered a delusion. Moreover, it is questionable whether polarization is the best way to get rid of white prejudice, though this is an argument better taken up elsewhere.

The black consciousness movement has surely been of immense importance to black people in Britain in helping them preserve a sense of dignity and self-respect in an unsupportive environment. A dark complexion, as an indicator of shared experience, can offer a basis for solidarity between two previous strangers (just as it can for whites in a black country). Yet the significance of such a colour has been insufficient to support any viable minority organizations on the stage of British party politics. There are categories of white people who have shared interests as consumers but do not organize to pursue these interests unless the producers choose to help them (in the way that public utilities such as the electricity boards support consumers' consultative councils). Ethnic minority members are, in a sense, a category of consumers who have established a great variety of representative bodies but none of them has been able to exercise any bargaining power. Their lack of success is to be understood as stemming not from any shortage of competence or commitment on the part of their members but from the general obstacles to collective action discussed in Mancur Olson's book and outlined in Chapter 2.

The earliest New Commonwealth immigrant political organization was the Indian Workers' Association (IWA) founded in Coventry in 1938. Further associations with similar names were formed in other towns in the 1950s, and in 1958 a national association was created to bring together the local societies. The IWAs have become the major political association of the Sikhs. After the Notting Hill disorders of 1959 the High Commission of the then federated government of the West Indies fostered the creation in London of the Standing Conference of West Indian Organizations, an umbrella body bringing together representatives of the various societies of people from the Caribbean. It has given evidence to a series of inquiries by the House of Commons Select Committee and Home Affairs Committee (in 1974–5 their representatives said that thirty-four or thirty-five organizations belonged to the Standing Conference and that they held meetings every month). Their example was followed in 1963 by a National Federation of Pakistani Associations in Great Britain (though it was a Standing Conference of Pakistani Associations which presented evidence to this Select Committee in 1974–5, along with a Federation of Bangladesh Associations in the United Kingdom).

The first organization to attempt to bring together all people of New Commonwealth origin was a welfare organization rather than a political one. It was the League of Coloured Peoples, founded in 1931 by Dr Harold Moody, a Jamaican medical practitioner. After the war, when the prospects for colonial independence brightened, the League functioned for a time as a body which arranged deputations to the Colonial Office on overseas issues, but it did not involve itself significantly in matters deriving from the settlement of people from Africa, the West Indies and South Asia. Around 1954–5 the League expired. There was a white-led organization at this time called Racial Unity which was active for a few years but it made little public impact and was not directly political.

After a brief visit to London by Dr Martin Luther King late in 1964, a new body was formed there called the Campaign Against Racial Discrimination; for three years it was a very effective pressure group, stating the case for legislation and advising on the form it might best take. CARD (as it was commonly known) was to be an umbrella organization bringing together representatives from minority associations and from its own branches in different parts of the country. It provided a platform on which people from different minorities, and reformers from the majority population, were, for a time, able to cooperate. But, writes Benjamin W. Heineman (1972: 101), a visitor from the United States who has published a reliable account of the venture, it proved much more difficult to recruit individual immigrants to membership than the more politically conscious organizers calculated. Immigrant organizations at both national and local levels were simply not strong enough to be able to play the parts envisaged for them. CARD did not develop as planned because the fundamental problems of motivating and uniting newcomers from three different cultural areas proved too difficult. After three years the organization foundered over issues of rhetoric rather than substance. In November 1967 a conference resolution was proposed that 'CARD, realizing that racialism, racial prejudice and racial discrimination are manifestations of imperialism, will fight against imperialism in all its forms by all the means at its disposal.' The opponents of this resolution argued that colonial freedom was a separate issue requiring its own separate organizations. To enlarge the purposes of CARD in this way would strain its pathetically small resources, divide its energies and split it politically. As *The Times* remarked, the danger for CARD was that if it committed itself to the proposed objective it would lose many friends at a crucial time for race relations in Britain, and on the eve of fresh legislation which it might hope to influence. But if it did not accept this resolution it would grievously divide its own membership (see Banton, 1972: 20–40). The break-up was not inevitable. A minority within the organization got its way because many of the black members, including the chairman, Dr David Pitt, were unable to withstand the call for black solidarity. Heineman's judgement (1972: 212) is that

> powerlessness perpetuated itself through faction . . . those with different theories about organizations and processes of change, representing tiny constituencies, contested for titular control of an essentially powerless institution that had almost no power in the general political world and little influence in its own universe, save force of personality or clarity of thought. Antagonism escalated and substantive work diminished as people were driven off (1972: 212).

This Gresham's law by which good people were driven out by bad organization has been a continuing theme in the history of the race relations industry.

CARD was a multi-racial organization. Other attempts have been made to establish organizations for minority members alone. One was the Racial Action Adjustment Society mentioned above, which was founded after a visit to Britain by the Afro-American black Muslim leader Michael X. When in 1974–5 the Select Committee enquired into the Organization of Race Relations Administration they received evidence from the Association of West Indian and Afro-Asian Minorities and from the Constituent Committee of the Proposed National Black People's Organization. The history of this last-named body has a special significance. In 1973 an official of the United Kingdom branch of the Calouste Gulbenkian Foundation indicated that the Foundation would be prepared to support a seminar on objectives and strategies in race relations policy, and sought the help of the Community Relations Commission. The proposals ran into criticism from people who thought it would be more useful to try to bring together minority views. A steering committee composed basically of ethnic minority members was formed. It staged a conference on Black People in Britain – The Way Forward which was held in London in January 1975. A verbatim report of the proceedings published under that title, and the annual reports of the Foundation, tell the story between them.

As the organizers sought to create a black peoples' movement, they wanted the conference to be representative of the various minorities in different parts of the country. If the meeting was to show results, careful preparation was necessary. So draft proposals for policy in the fields of education, employment, housing, and anti-discriminatory legislation were circulated and participants allocated to study groups charged with providing guidance for further policy-making. This strategy met with only very limited success. Some delegates wished to voice their suspicions of the Foundation's role, others of the steering committee's lack of popular mandate. They insisted that if there was to be any further activity it must be representative of grass roots organizations up and down the country. The organizers did not want the conference to discuss resolutions from the floor but the participants overruled them, with the result that a series was passed, censuring the organizers, demanding the repeal of the 1971 Immigration Act, supporting the cause of a man on whom a deportation order had been served, expressing solidarity with the liberation struggles of the peoples of Asia, Africa, the Caribbean and Latin America, favouring the establishment of credit unions, insisting upon an immediate end to police harassment, demanding the payment of £5,000 millions in reparation, etc. At the end of the day, at least the proposal for a constituent committee had survived and this body, with a further grant from Gulbenkian (in all, the Foundation paid out £27,526), held another conference in Birmingham in July 1977. On this occasion, despite determined attempts to disrupt the meeting, the overwhelming majority of the 400 participants approved the adoption of the proposed constitution for a National Organization of African, Asian and Caribbean People (NOAACP); yet this body did not manage to convene a second annual general meeting.

The help which the Foundation gave to this venture can be seen as a recognition of the thesis (well expressed by Heineman, 1972: 225–9) that many of the ethnic minorities' troubles stemmed from their powerlessness as a collectivity. If they could be helped to establish an effective bargaining agency this would be in the interest of the majority as well as of the minorities. The attempt was over-ambitious and it failed. It was based on the assumption that all who suffer from racial discrimination should be able to unite in opposing it although their views as to the best strategies diverged sharply. All non-whites were to be brought together as 'black people', but the eventual choice of another name demonstrated that the designation 'black people' did not command general approval. The objective was to create a representative body, yet there was no method by which representatives could be elected locally. The participants wanted the leaders to be accountable to them, but they were not concerned so much that the leaders should be accountable for the way they spent the organization's money as for the demands to be made upon the government. There was no structure which would enable the leaders to offer anything in return for any concessions they might secure. In view of these difficulties and the rarity of foundations willing to play the fairy-godmother role, it is unlikely that any similar venture could succeed where this one failed. The history of the organization demonstrated again both the powerlessness of the non-whites as a section of the British population and the difficulty experienced by many leading members of that section in coming to terms with the realities of their predicament.

One reason why New Commonwealth immigrants have given little support to organizations founded in their name has been that to start with many of them have planned to return to the countries from which they came. Their political interests have been concentrated on those countries. Lord Pitt tells a story of the time when he was, as Dr David Pitt, the Labour Party candidate in the 1970 by-election in Clapham (an election he believed he could have won had there been more time for him to become personally known to the voters). Outside an underground station he introduced himself to a Jamaican woman who reacted with a note of slight alarm and disapproval when she learned that this big black man was seeking election to the House of Commons: 'Me, I came here to get some milk', she said, 'not to try and take the cow!'

Those who did not plan to return may well have been too busy establishing themselves in Britain to have had much time to spare for political activities. Many were not concerned to see that their names were on the electoral register. Some may have felt, and still feel, that it is little use organizing politically since the ethnic minorities are too small in total number and too dispersed to be able to influence the outcome.

Some may fear, too, that were they to influence the outcome it would only result in a white backlash. The belief that the British electoral system is so structured that the minorities have little chance of gaining representation is indeed well founded. Ivor Crewe in a recent analysis of electoral data (1983) maintains that not only are the minorities politically weak but that it is hard to imagine a political system less well designed to represent the specific concerns of small and unpopular ethnic minorities. A separate ethnic party could nowhere gather enough votes to have an influence upon national politics. It is extremely difficult for a minority member to obtain a party nomination for a winnable seat (though Jewish parliamentarians far exceed their proportion in the general population). Two-party systems are structurally incapable of representing the exclusive interests of small minorities because they have to compete for the floating voter. The ethnic minorities are unable to influence the result by tactical voting in marginal constituencies because too many English voters would be antagonized by any open attempt to solicit an ethnic vote. The typical British elector, says Crewe, is implacably opposed to further coloured immigration, regards strict immigration control rather than inner city aid as the key to good race relations, and considers that action to promote racial equality has already gone far enough (in 1979 30 per cent of those polled answered that 'recent attempts to ensure equality for coloured people' had 'gone too far' and 29 per cent that they had 'not gone far enough'). Operating with a loose definition of racism, Crewe concludes that 'racists easily outnumber Asians and West Indians combined among the electorate, and indeed among Labour partisans.' Either of the main parties can pick up votes by appealing to racial prejudices.

> The stark truth is that the ethnic communities must very largely rely on the commitment and goodwill of whites to dissolve prejudice, eliminate discrimination, guarantee civil rights and abolish poverty . . . Rioting is certainly more likely to attract publicity, official enquiries and research. Whether it is any more effective in obtaining commitment and goodwill remains to be seen. This author doubts it (Crewe, 1983: 280).

The riots in the United States in 1967 reflected an Afro-American mobilization movement that had been gathering strength amongst most sections of the black population during the preceding ten years. The commission of investigation said of the rioters that 'rather than rejecting the American system, they were anxious to obtain a place for themselves in it'. Their attacks were directed at local symbols of the white authority and property that seemed to stand in their way. By drawing national attention to the consequences of three centuries of racial injustice, the riots added substantially to the bargaining strength of black representatives and agencies. The parallels between these disorders and the 1981 riots in British cities attracted much attention, but the differences are also important. As recent immigrants, New Commonwealth minority members in many respects resemble Hispanic-Americans more closely than Afro-Americans, and their internal differentiation is at least as great as that of Hispanic-Americans. Whether the United States riots were race riots is arguable, but the British ones certainly were not. Lord Scarman said of Brixton 'the riots were essentially an outburst of anger and resentment by young black people against the police'. Though young blacks played a crucial part in the disorders in many cities, at times there seem to have been as many or more white rioters and looters. A few whites have invoked the threat of future riots as a form of negative-sum bargaining on behalf of the minorities, but minority representatives have not wished to identify themselves or their groups with this kind of action; they may have concluded that were they to do so this would only weaken their bargaining power.

Experience so far suggests that while ethnic minorities in Britain may be able, for at least a generation, to advance their shared interests by collective action on specific issues at the local level, they will not in this way be able to make any progress at the national level. If present trends continue even local action will become increasingly difficult as more people of New Commonwealth origin come to identify themselves with the majority society.

5

The public good

Once legislation has won public acceptance it requires a conscious effort to understand why it was so difficult to get that legislation enacted in the first place. The benefits of the 1956 Clean Air Act are now taken for granted. That there should be some kind of law against racial discrimination is also now beyond challenge, but getting the 1965 and 1968 Race Relations Acts onto the statute book was nevertheless a remarkable achievement at the time, especially in view of the wide-spread belief that legislation was either unnecessary or likely to be positively harmful. No minister could bring to parliament a bill to penalize discrimination in employment or housing unless it had the support of the ministers responsible for those departments; they in turn felt obliged to consult the organizations with which they had to work; the employers and unions in the one case, and the local authorities in the other. The Labour Party, in its 1964 election manifesto, had indeed promised support for legislation. Once in office it brought in the 1965 act penalizing discrimination in places of public resort (like hotels, dance halls and public transport), with the Race Relations Board as an enforcement agency. The incitement of racial hatred also became a criminal offence. These were important steps but they did not touch the main inequalities of opportunity.

They were followed by what Nicholas Deakin has called 'the liberal hour' for race relations policies. It started in December 1965 when Roy Jenkins was appointed Home Secretary, and was partly his creation. Taking advantage of his opportunities, Jenkins made this one of those periods in which 'public men of all shades of opinion, from radical to conservative, accept the necessity of a movement in policy on a social problem issue, in a liberal direction' (Rose, 1969: 10). Among the features of this period should be counted, first, the impulse given by Jenkins; secondly, the uncovering of the incidence of racial discrimination in employment, housing, and financial services like insurance, which made possible the enactment of the much stronger Race Relations Act of 1968; thirdly, the transformation of the National Committee into the Community Relations Commission and the local committees into community relations councils and the declaration of government policy that 'no artificial barrier of race or colour should prevent any individual from developing his abilities to the full and from acquiring both the economic and social status to which his skills entitle him . . . the major effort must be directed towards ensuring that the children of immigrants, who have either been born or received their education here, are treated on exactly the same terms as all other citizens and that their colour of skin becomes totally irrelevant'; fourthly, the inclusion in the Local Government Act 1966 of Section 11, empowering the Home Secretary to pay grants in respect of the employment of staff by those local authorities who have had to make special provision 'in consequence of the presence within their areas of substantial numbers of immigrants from the Commonwealth whose language or customs differ from those of the community'; these actions can be seen as an acceptance by the government of the proposition that racial harmony is a public good. The cross-party interest in such matters was also evinced by the establishment, in 1968, of the House of Commons Select Committee on Race Relations and Immigration to review policies in these two areas. The liberal hour ended when Jenkins left the Home Office and, shortly afterwards, the government enacted the 1968 Commonwealth Immigration bill to withdraw immigration rights from brown-skinned British subjects in East Africa.

In the aftermath of the bitter debates over the 1962 act and the white paper, the political climate with respect to race relations was pessimistic and shamefaced, because the issues were all conceived within the framework of immigration control. Jenkins' task was to change that climate and to make use of the sentiments of common citizenship and human equality which had been subordinated to short-term interests. He took over a department responsible for the negative functions of administering the 1962 act and of maintaining public order. He hoped (vainly) to counterbalance the negative aspect by having the Home Office made responsible for coordinating the government's policies for race relations. It was more difficult to deal with the Minister of Labour who, both in public and private, was a persistent critic of his proposals, and the Minister of Housing who, according to Deakin, was not only sceptical of the case for further legislation but was complacent and negative on the broader issues. (Deakin's account of this period is convincing in its detail and persuasive in its judgements; this chapter's indebtedness to it should be apparent at many points.)

In the early months of 1965 the political balance was delicate and immigration still a threatening issue. Therefore Jenkins waited until after the election (when Labour was returned with an increased majority) to make the first of his major speeches about race relations and to set about changing the climate. That first speech has been quoted, times beyond number, for his statement that he did not regard integration 'as meaning the loss, by immigrants of their own national characteristics and culture. I do not think that we need in this country a "melting-pot" . . . I define integration, therefore, not as a flattening process of assimilation but as equal opportunity, accompanied by cultural diversity, in an atmosphere of mutual tolerance. This is the goal' (Patterson, 1969: 112–13). As a political statement, Jenkins' declaration was appreciated for its sensitivity to minority feelings and its emphasis upon the moral value of tolerance. It made integration sound more acceptable by contrasting it with a 'straight line' conception of assimilation, something which, had it ever occurred, would indeed have been a flattening process. Jenkins went on to say of the immigrants 'Most of those who have come here in the past decade and a half are accepting an unwritten, unspoken assumption. They have come expecting to do only the most menial jobs, because they are better than no jobs at home.' He implied that they were willing to put up with some discrimination provided they could count on British readiness to accept their children as full citizens. In a subsequent speech he went on to express pleasure 'that we appear to have put behind us the sterile debate about the precise level of the flow of immigration'.

Jenkins promised to provide a positive lead through non-legislative action by central government, both as an employer and by inserting non-discrimination clauses in governing contracts. His minister of state in the House of Lords reviewed a whole series of such actions, ending with a new note of optimism and pride: 'We shall make a great success of this policy – a success which I think will be an example to the world.' To repair the deficiencies of the 1965 act Jenkins needed evidence about the nature and extent of discrimination and, if it was to fit into the parliamentary timetable, he needed it quickly. The Home Office could not assemble this; it had to be prepared by an independent body; if it demonstrated substantial discrimination then press publicity might help the Home Secretary mobilize public sympathy for his policy. So by June of 1966 the National Committee for Commonwealth Immigrants and the Race Relations Board were planning a study of discrimination in employment, housing and financial services (motor insurance and car hire) to be undertaken by Political and Economic Planning (PEP, an independent research institute now part of the Policy Studies Institute). The initiative came from Jenkins. When the report appeared early in 1967 it showed that the incidence of discrimination was higher than generally expected (even by members of the minorities) and that, since more discrimination was experienced by the more Anglicized and more skilled minority members, the continuation of present policies would bring no alleviation. Test applications showed that most of the private housing market, particularly in rented accommodation, was closed to black and Asian applicants. If they were at so great a disadvantage in this crucial sphere, they would never be able to catch up those who resembled them in every way other than skin colour.

The report got a very sympathetic reception from the press because it touched upon the most sensitive point: the ordinary Briton's pride in his country and its belief in being fair. The reaction in all the major newspapers was that the report had revealed an intolerable situation calling for urgent remedial action. This gave Jenkins political support in addition to the hard evidence of the study itself. It could be coupled with the arguments of the first report of the Race Relations Board, since Mr Mark Bonham Carter had accepted the chairmanship only on condition that after a year's operation he should be free to state a case for the extension of the act's scope and a revision of the board's powers. He seized his opportunity, presenting a closely argued case in his first report. The Confederation of British Industry and the Trades Union Council softened their opposition to legislation in just the merest fraction, but the overall change was enough for Jenkins to persuade his cabinet colleagues, and by the early summer the crucial decisions had been taken.

This was only just in time, for the government's position was weakening. In April 1967 Labour lost control of the Greater London Council for the first time in thirty years. It suffered catastrophic defeats in the borough council elections of the following month. It was losing authority at home and failing overseas, where United States involvement in Vietnam cast a dark shadow. On specifically racial issues the liberal centre was disintegrating because, on the one hand, it had been unable to allay white fears about immigration, while on the other hand, the growth of black consciousness in the United States encouraged the polarization of opinion in much the same way as the immigration control lobby, even if for different reasons. Deakin believes that the 1967 riots in United States cities undermined much of the effect of the work Jenkins had put into the timing and content of his announcement about the pending legislation. As the previous chapter has explained, it was at just this time that the Campaign Against Racial Discrimination, which since 1964 had been an unusually successful pressure group, was killed by an ill-considered attempt to make it part of a militant anti-imperialist campaign.

Jenkins maintained a positive and constructive tone but by the end of November he had been succeeded as Home Secretary by James Callaghan. Mark Bonham Carter has testified that Callaghan did not understand that the 1968 Race Relations Act was meant to be the foundation on which further positive action in the field was to be based (*The Observer*, 20 December 1981). Callaghan took the new bill through the House of Commons but he spoiled its effect, so Bonham Carter claims, by his response to the crisis of the Kenya Asians. When Kenya became independent they had been given British citizenship. Iain Macleod, the former Colonial Secretary, wrote 'We did it. We meant to do it. And in the event we had no other choice.' In 1967 the Kenyan government passed a law which meant that non-Kenyan citizens could work and live in Kenya only on a temporary basis. So some of the Asians who had not taken out Kenyan nationality came to Britain. Between 1962 and Kenyan independence such persons had been subject to the British 1962 Immigration Act. After Kenyan independence they had passports from the British High Commissioner in Nairobi, not from any colonial government. Should they, nevertheless, be subject to the 1962 controls? The British government, despite criticism far more bitter than in 1962, passed a new law to make them so. Deakin contends that it was unnecessary and that had they reaffirmed the Kenyan Asians' right of entry, few of them would have chosen to exercise it. As it was, that debate was followed by the Ugandan tragedy when President Amin expelled that country's Asians. Then after April 1968 any constructive discussion of race relations policy in a political forum was rendered almost impossible by Enoch Powell's intervention, though he claimed to be discussing not race relations but immigration. The climate was once again pessimistic – but no longer shamefaced.

Could another Home Secretary have done more than Jenkins? It may appear very elementary, but it is worth recalling that a government's powers are primarily legislative and financial. Ministers also have a great deal of influence. The priorities of a department of central government can be greatly affected by the personal interests of particular ministers. Many people outside the government can be persuaded by ministers to attach greater significance to matters they have not previously treated as important (some of them perhaps because they hope one day to see their names in the honours list). Governments cannot dictate. They cannot simply order that members of racial minorities shall receive their fair share on the job market. This is, after all, a market; one in which a great range of considerations apart from racial ones affect who gets what. Most jobs are in the private sector. Who gets them depends upon employers and, in some cases, unions. The scope for discrimination may depend upon how competitive the market is. The government's powers with respect to jobs in the public sector are greater, but they are still very limited when it comes to the health service, post office, telecommunications, railways, electricity and gas boards, defence establishments, coal mines, and so on. Who gets those jobs is almost equally beyond a minister's control because so much of the power he might exercise has already been delegated to boards representing various interests (many of them regional or local) and bodies of specialist knowledge.

In a 100 per cent competitive labour market an employer who discriminated against a worker or a candidate for promotion because that worker was female, or dark-complexioned, or had a physical handicap irrelevant to the job, would make less profit and, in the long run, be driven out of business. Since there are no markets like this, other measures are necessary to restrict the grosser kinds of unfairness in hiring and firing. The law can (and now does) provide for tribunals to adjudicate upon accusations of this kind, but these tribunals can be effective only because they now have the support of employers' associations and unions which nominate suitable people to sit and adjudicate as tribunal members.

Similar arguments apply to housing and other sectors in which policies of non-discrimination are wanted. The central government owns relatively few houses. Most dwellings are privately owned or rented though about a quarter are owned by local authorities. These bodies guard their independence irrespective of their party composition; they insist that they should be responsive to their electorates and to their local circumstances. Their policies for house-building and for deciding how to allocate tenancies between competing applicants vary from one locality to another. The central government appointed a committee under Professor Barry Cullingworth which in 1969 recommended that authorities keep records of the ethnic origin of people on their waiting lists and of people rehoused through these lists on clearance schemes, or because of special need. If they did so they could then monitor the outcomes and look for any possible sources of discrimination. Despite this recommendation there have been instances of housing officials assuring research workers that the Cullingworth committee advised against the keeping of ethnic records. Sociological research has demonstrated over and over again that in the course of implementation policies are modified bit by bit by officials and that those in contact with the public at the 'bottom' of the structure find ways of modifying them so as to minimize change to their customary practices. Central government bodies, like parliamentary committees, can uncover such failures in policy implementation and press local authorities to rectify them, but the responsibility for doing so must rest with those who employ the officials in question.

Any Home Secretary is confronted with problems, like prison overcrowding, for which he is responsible even though he can exercise no control over their causes (in this case, the level of crime and the sentencing policies of the courts). Racial relations have presented a greater difficulty because their features do not fit the structure of public administration. Some of the problems as these might be seen from the ministries of employment and housing have been hinted at, but there were also those associated with education, health, social services, the police and so on, each of which had its own division of responsibility between central and local government. A policy for race relations could bring no quick results and was more likely to lose votes than win them. It was not something most ministers would see as offering an opportunity for them to improve their political reputation, so they would give it low priority. A Home Secretary who decided to act had to create an organization that would stimulate and coordinate action in a great variety of circumstances. In the early years it had to be an organization that related to people rather than to official departments, for it was the same people who suffered from discrimination or disadvantage in the various sectors. The problems came together in their lives not in the bureaucratic categories, and it was their opportunities which had to be improved if the future was to be brighter. When Roy Jenkins became Home Secretary a National Committee for Commonwealth Immigrants with a distinguished membership was already in existence. (The readiness of the Archbishop of Canterbury to serve as its chairman gave a major boost to the community relations movement; some comparable action by an establishment figure after the riots in 1958 would have been even more timely.) The committee was a multi-purpose body devised (i) to advise the government, and (ii) to develop community activity at local level wherever commonwealth immigrants were settled. This second function stemmed from the concept of the liaison committee which provided a setting for local officials, minority representatives, and members of the white majority concerned for good relations to meet and communicate more effectively. If this concept was to work a very delicate balance had to be maintained. In 1967 the general secretary reported 'A body dedicated simultaneously to "liaison", conciliation, the eradication of injustices and the propagation of a new spirit, is constantly confronted by choices which seem impossible to make.' This is the theme of priorities which runs as a fault line of failure through the history of official policy since 1965 despite the efforts of Jenkins and Bonham Carter who identified it as the main weakness in their programmes. It was bound to be a weakness for the first ten years but as circumstances changed it could have been substantially remedied.

The central task confronting anyone who would combat racial discrimination can be compared with that facing the campaigner who wants to persuade others to stop smoking. He has to persuade others to place a higher value upon their health than they place upon the pleasure they obtain from smoking (alternatively, he could try to persuade them to set a higher value on the other uses to which they could put the money they currently spend on tobacco). The campaigner against racial discrimination has (i) to persuade administrators to put a higher value on the anti-discriminatory objectives related to their work, and (ii) to persuade members of the public to set more value on the reduction of racial discrimination (so that their children can live in a more harmonious society) than they presently place upon the convenience of continuing in the ways to which they are accustomed. In pursuit of (i) the central agency (the NCCI or CRC) had to act in a 'staff' capacity in relation to the 'line' responsibilities of the officials in the ministries and local authorities – with the qualification that they might have to press their advice upon an unwilling listener. For this operation a multi-purpose agency was needed. To have created a host of smaller agencies in all the various bodies it was hoped to influence would have been extravagant and productive of confusion. With such varied functions and tasks the central agency was bound to have problems in deciding priorities and in keeping to them. The main error was that it had no philosophy about whether, when, and how, to transfer responsibilities to officials in the line of command in the ministries and local authorities.

The origin of the National Committee for Commonwealth Immigrants lay in the creation of a clearing house to advise and assist local voluntary liaison committees. In its first report the reconstituted committee said it had

> to steer a somewhat complex course. It is engaged in the work of community relations in the broadest sense and must take care never to build up a separate structure of services, and therefore a separate position, for the immigrant. At the same time it must do everything possible to reverse the undoubtedly negative trends of today and to ensure that the newcomers and their children become an integral part of the community (Patterson, 1969: 122).

The committee's function of advising the government proved a source of strain on both sides. A deputation saw the Prime Minister to dispute part of the 1965 white paper referring to immigration, particularly procedures on admission and the right of appeal. A further deputation on behalf of the voluntary liaison committees queried cases of refusal of admission. There were additional deputations to both ministers and an exchange of correspondence with the Prime Minister, largely on the position of the Kenyan Asians and the potential effectiveness of the then forthcoming Race Relations Bill 1968. Later a public statement was issued declaring opposition to Section 1 of the Commonwealth Immigration Act, 1968 (Abbott, 1971: 295–6). The committee appointed a series of panels concerned with education, employment, housing, health, children, community relations, training, public relations and information, and legal questions. They attracted a wide range of well-qualified people to serve on these, thus involving a substantial number of influential persons in the work of the committee. Partly because of the diffuseness of the task with which they were presented many of these panels lost momentum. Coordinating the local voluntary liaison committees was difficult because voluntary bodies are necessarily more independent. The role of the full-time, paid liaison officer was the more demanding because it was new and there were no settled expectations as to how it should be discharged. The committee was increasingly involved with local organizations but its difficulties were increased by the way this function was harnessed to the political one.

Some activists and critics wanted the NCCI to be first and foremost a political representative of the ethnic minorities; these minorities could not represent themselves politically in any effective way and did not have the funds and public position of the NCCI; they believed that the minorities required above all some organ that could be their national voice and could help them organize at the local level, so it was not surprising that they hoped to fashion the NCCI to their purposes. Michael and Ann Dummett (whose criticisms have been mentioned earlier) contend that the minorities could well have developed their own organization, and that, in alliance with white anti-racialists, there could have been a vibrant civil rights movement had the NCCI not diverted the energies of potential leaders into the new bureaucracy. The critics were over-sanguine in their expectations of what might have been but the studies of the local committees at this time (see Abbott, 1971: 312–17) show some of the difficulties of creating a new institutional structure that is expected to serve many purposes simultaneously. Writing at the end of the 1960s, Simon Abbott (1971: 322) concluded that it could not be proved that the NCCI had improved the position of the ethnic minorities in any clearly distinguishable manner but that this was not to say that the situation might not have been still worse had it not been established.

The Race Relations Act 1968 replaced the NCCI with the Community Relations Commission. Under this act increased funds were provided for local organizations concerned with community relations (subsequently called community relations councils). The commission's advisory functions at the national level were refined and diminished, bringing it more closely under the Home Secretary whose approval was required for appointing certain advisory committees. Its function as a body organizing community relations work throughout the country was strengthened. The commission's first chairman was Frank Cousins, a former trade union leader who had for a short while served as a cabinet minister.

In its first annual report, that for 1968–9, the commission interpreted its title as indicating that it had to concern itself with what it called 'the host community' as well as the immigrants. Looking back on its predecessor's work it stated that the NCCI's most notable achievement was no doubt the part it had played in the preparation of the 1968 Race Relations Act and in assembling 'the whole machinery of a national movement for encouraging the establishment of good community relations at the local level'. Questioned by the parliamentary Select Committee the chairman said 'members of my commission . . . have understood the difference between . . . us [over] the immigration policy of the country; that is determined by you people, in a political judgement'.

Nevertheless, the commission did not get off to a happy start. After just over a year its senior administrative officer (a man with consider-able experience of official administration) resigned. He published an article expressing disappointment: 'The Commission has yet to make its mark. No striking initiative, not even a memorable phrase, has yet emerged.' John Reddaway (1970: 213) went on to explain 'Part of the trouble is that in the Act the Commission's terms of reference are so broadly written as to encourage expectations which cannot possibly be fulfilled.' The act contained some governmental window-dressing which excused these expectations, but the real explanation of the com-mission's failure was simpler. 'It . . . has not so far managed to equip itself with administrative machinery capable of discharging its func-tions with tolerable efficiency . . . like its predecessor [the commission] has been plagued by poor staff relations, by rapid turn-over in the holders of the subordinate professional posts, and by difficulty in filling these posts.' He noted 'a disagreeable atmosphere infecting not only personal relations within the office but also the conduct of business with other organizations and individuals outside with whom there should be a relationship of confidence and cordial cooperation'.

At the beginning of 1971, Mark Bonham Carter moved across from the Race Relations Board to become chairman of the Community Relations Commission. He declared

> The most immediate task of the CRC is to get community relations in a multi-racial society higher on the agenda: higher on the agenda of central and local government, of employers and trade unionists, of teachers, social workers and voluntary organizations . . . our task is to identify problems and persuade others to tackle them . . . The Commission has still to attain a position where it is expected to speak to and be listened to by those who exercise power: it has still to persuade the majority to do what they ought to be doing in any case. (Report, 1971–2: 2 and 5)

In subsequent reports the commission stated that 'the history of immigration in this country is proving inexorably that – like the decaying city centres – community relations do not take care of themselves'. Government intervention was essential (Report, 1972–3: 28). Despite their belief that it was not the job of the community relations organization to make up for the deficiencies of other bodies, the CRC decided against any policy of transferring responsibilities in the belief that it was best to preserve the autonomy of local councils. The balance tipped in favour of the view that the commission and the councils should serve as a voice for the minorities; thus the 1974–5 report described the CRC's strategy as:

(i)   to develop and maintain contact with ethnic minority groups;
(ii) to identify the needs of these groups and propose how they should be met;
(iii) to press government and other institutions to meet these needs and provide the resources to do so; and, in the last resort, to demonstrate by means of pilot projects ways and means of meeting these needs; and
(iv) to develop techniques for monitoring the progress of community relations.

Mention was made earlier of the establishment of the House of Commons Select Committee on Race Relations and Immigration in the 1968–9 session of parliament. This committee chose first to investigate the problems of coloured school leavers. It called for evidence from central and local government departments with responsibilities in the field of youth employment and invited evidence from all other bodies and individuals who believed they had something to contribute. Many of the organizations and individuals which sent in memoranda were invited to appear in person before the committee to speak and be questioned. Since the committee convened in a variety of cities throughout England and Wales as well as in London, its impact was considerable. Local authority departments treated with respect and urgency a request for memoranda from a committee of the House of Commons, memoranda moreover on which they could be subject to public examination. Though reports of select committees were not usually debated in parliament, they were substantial and authoritative documents. Central government departments felt obliged to issue, in due course, further reports on the action they were taking in response to the committee's recommendations. As appendices to their reports the committee published volumes reprinting the evidence they had received and verbatim accounts of their examination of witnesses. Thus for a period of ten years the Select Committee was a major vehicle for the making of government policy in its special field. Its reports were as follows:

1968–9   Problems of Coloured School Leavers
1970–1   Housing
1971–2   Police/Immigrant Relations
1972–3   Education
1974   Employment
1974–5   The Organization of Race Relations Administration
1976–7   The West Indian Community
1977–8   Immigration

With the return to power of a Labour government after the election of 1974, and with Roy Jenkins as Home Secretary once again, there was a second spell of liberalism, more cautious than before. The government announced its intention of reviewing the race relations legislation. It intended to introduce legislation against discrimination on grounds of sex and planned to harmonize, and possibly amalgamate, the powers and procedures for dealing with both forms of discrimination. The Select Committee played their part in this review by undertaking their own examination of the Organization of Race Relations Administration. They examined evidence from three main sources. First, government departments: the Home Office, the Department of Education and Science, the Department of the Environment, the Department of Employment and the Association of Municipal Authorities submitted memoranda and their representatives were questioned in public. Several other bodies submitted memoranda only, including the Department of Health and Social Security, the Civil Service Department, the Scottish Office and the Association of County Councils. Secondly, there were witnesses from bodies concerned with community relations: The Race Relations Board, the Community Relations Commission, The National Association of Community Relations Councils, the Association of Scientific, Technical and Managerial Staffs (a trade union to which many community relations staff belonged) and the Runnymede Trust (an independent information agency). Thirdly, bodies representing ethnic minority groups: the West Indian Standing Conference, the Standing Conference of Asian Organizations, the Standing Conference of Pakistan Organizations, the Federation of Bangladesh Associations, the Indian Workers' Association, the Supreme Council of Sikhs, The Board of Deputies of British Jews, the Association of West Indian, Asian, and Afro-Asian Minorities and the Constituent Committee of the Proposed National Black People's organization. The evidence from these three sources will be considered in turn.

When a Select Committee examines the activities of a government department a minister sometimes comes to present the department's case but usually it has to be represented by civil servants. They can speak only for policies which have been agreed by ministers and about matters of factual information. Since civil servants are moved from one department to another to broaden their experience, those who attend to be questioned may not have had any lengthy experience of matters under examination. Sometimes they have to adopt a defensive posture. Thus the Home Office had declared that with respect to community relations 'The role of the Home Office is to take the lead within Government in promoting the development of concerted policies — based, as far as possible, on common principles. These principles are at present under review.' The Select Committee chairman accepted that new principles might be advanced but could see no reason for uncertainty about those which guided action in the present. How could the department review its principles if it did not know what its principles were? All the poor official could say was that they were perhaps a little sanguine in implying that there were any common principles, but that the recognition that racial problems were rooted in the wider problems of urban deprivation might be one of them. Certainly when, later in the year, the Home Office produced its white paper, *Racial Discrimination*, it had advanced no further in the search for such principles.

When asked if it was not the case that the Home Office had very little control and not much knowledge of what was going on in the realm of race relations, its representative had to agree that it did not know a great deal of what was going on and did not have the capacity to do so. But it had 'a very large number of reports and recommendations totalling at the moment something of the order of 300' touching upon education, housing, social services and employment which it was coordinating in the attempt to evolve common policies for government departments. (This list was published as an appendix but the Home Office was unable to answer the Member of Parliament who enquired how many had been implemented and how many rejected.) The official representatives also had a rough time when questioned about their use of the funds allocated them for research – 'It is a pitiful amount on research is it not?' 'It does not put the Government in a very strong position in saying that they think research is important in this field, does it?' asked the chairman. The Home Office representatives could not dissent. They were probably relieved when the MPs switched their fire to another target and one asked if they did not agree that such improvements in race relations as had taken place had been because of the contact between people and that which had been brought about by the race relations industry had been 'very very small indeed'.

The sharpest criticism of the government's record came from the Runnymede Trust which contrasted the active role of the Home Office in the field of immigration control with its passivity on the domestic front. The Home Office suggested that the responsibility for policy-making lay with the Community Relations Commission but that body only advised the government. The government had to be in a position to assess the adequacy of the advice it received. Apparently the Home Office still could not do this. Nor could it provide leadership to other departments, as could be seen by comparing the performance of the Department of Employment (which was now at last getting a move on) with the Department of the Environment which had neglected race relations. (The previous month the Select Committee asked a representative of that department why it was the only one not to have replied to a report from the committee. The official said 'We have been working on it for three and a half years. I am extremely sorry it has taken so long.' Even when the Department produced its white paper on *Race Relations and Housing* it still, according to the Race Relations Board, provided insufficient guidance to local authorities).

On research the Runnymede Trust was equally scathing. They said:

> It is an open secret that the Home Office has made so little use of the services and advice of its own Advisory Committee that the members saw little point in continuing . . . The reluctance of the Home Office to encourage the number of research ideas put forward by members of the Committee can hardly be attributed to a belief that the amount of research already in existence was adequate.

(The author was a member of this committee. It is his impression that the failure of the committee stemmed primarily from the policy vacuum, since any research conducted on government funds had to be relevant to official policy; the vacuum was not due to any illiberalism on the part of the officials but to their genuine puzzlement about how to formulate a policy that would move on from *Colour and Citizenship*; the unofficial members of the committee understood too little of the operation of government departments to overcome the bureaucratic hesitations and they failed to press with sufficient vigour their enquiries into the government's own role as an employer and contractor.)

The Trust maintained that 'the critical failure has been not to define the nature of Government concern with race relations, not to clarify the objectives of policy and not to assess the scope and limits of potential Government failure . . . there has been no driving force at the centre. Everyone has thought that because you had the Community Relations Commission you had a policy.' But this was a period in which Home Office officials were asking people like the specialists of the Runnymede Trust for advice as to what form a policy might take and they were getting very little constructive help in return. To be told that 'A Bill of Rights – or even more radically – a United Kingdom Federal Constitution may be necessary if the British system is properly to face the challenge of the new minorities', was, from the standpoint of even a senior Home Office administrator, to be told that no policy-making at the level with which he was concerned was going to be of much use.

The Community Relations Commission had to be more circumspect in its criticism of governmental inactivity. Its chairman reiterated that the government should place the promotion of racial harmony higher on its agenda; it should serve a good example by its own practice in the civil service, by leaning on the nationalized industries, exercising its own powers when drawing up contracts and monitoring policies of equal opportunity. Subsequently, the commission submitted an additional memorandum on the government's role in race relations which could well have been adopted as a formulation of the sort of policy that everyone seemed to be seeking. The commission had submitted eight reports to the Home Secretary but only once had he asked them to investigate a problem on his behalf. Too many recommendations, from the Select Committee and other bodies, seemed to get lost in the governmental apparatus.

In the evidence relating to the operation of bodies like the commission which were responsible for promoting racial harmony, the theme which came through most strongly was the question of minority representation. The National Association of Community Relations Councils (NACRC) said that 'the black ethnic groups feel a great isolation from their local host communities, their local community relations councils and they particularly feel that they have no representative institutions or are not adequately represented on the existing central institutions'. Mr Bonham Carter had said 'We do not claim to speak on their [the ethnic minorities'] behalf, nor do I think that we should do so.' He acknowledged that a frequent criticism was that white people were a majority influence on the councils. The NACRC wanted a pressure group. Drawing a comparison with the Child Poverty Action Group, they observed 'they get a modicum of success because there are regulations about social security that they can refer to. They can put their interpretation on them as opposed to the interpretation of an officer. There is something concrete to work to. This does not exist in community relations.' To this the chairman of the committee replied that the community relations council was the sort of forum in which pressure groups might exercise pressure. Witnesses were also concerned about the long-standing problems of who should be the employers of community relations officers and the division of functions and spending between local councils and the central commission. The impression conveyed, certainly by the NACRC, was one of frustration at every hand.

The bodies representing, or claiming to represent, the ethnic minorities, were agreed on one thing. They all (apart from the Board of Deputies of British Jews) wanted any new central agency for race relations to include someone from their own minority or for the membership of it to be in part representative of the ethnic minorities. As might be expected there were differences of opinion in that the Bangladeshis said 'a West Indian cannot understand our problem, neither can he communicate with us' whereas others considered that what all non-white people had in common was more important than what differentiated the various minorities.

Having reviewed this evidence the Select Committee declared in its report that 'What is needed, above everything else, is a clear and demonstrable Government commitment to equal rights.' To further this they proposed the appointment of a minister of state for equal rights in the Home Office and the creation of an equal rights commission for the enforcement of the legislation against sexual discrimination and racial discrimination. The Race Relations Board and the Community Relations Commission would be merged in this new body which would take over the employment of community relations officers, though local authorities would still be expected to support these. The establishments of the Home Office, Department of Employment, Department of Education and Science, Department of Environment, Department of Health and Social Security and Civil Service Department were to be increased to permit the appointment of specialist race relations staff. The CSD was to monitor, by records and surveys, the progress of equal opportunities policies in the civil service.

Later in 1975 the government published a white paper, *Racial Discrimination*, in which, among other things, it declared that 'That Government has a special responsibility as an employer.' With the full support of civil service staff representatives, it had stated that there should be no discrimination in recruitment, training or promotion.

> Since 1969 all Government contracts have contained a standard clause requiring contractors in the United Kingdom to conform to the provisions of the Race Relations Act 1968 relating to discrimination in employment and to take all reasonable steps to ensure that their employees and sub-contractors do the same . . . it is intended that [in future] the contractor will provide on request to the Department of Employment such information about its employment policies and practices as the Department may reasonably require.

(The Race Relations Board were disappointed that no stronger action was planned. In their 1971–2 report they had recommended that contractors should be under a positive obligation to provide equal opportunity and produce evidence of steps taken.)

In the following year the government replied to the Select Committee's recommendations. They had decided against having a single commission to enforce both the sexual discrimination and the racial discrimination laws. They noted that the Runnymede Trust had proposed a community relations inspectorate to administer, from the Home Office, a national service. The Race Relations Board had also observed that such a rearrangement could bring powerful advantages in increased professionalism, influence and effectiveness. The Home Office replied that they lacked the expertise which such proposals envisaged and that others would resent such an infringement upon their independence. They went on to comment on the committee's forty-six new recommendations.

The Race Relations Act 1976 was a much more substantial statute than its predecessors, providing increased powers against discriminatory practices and placing upon local authorities a duty to see that their functions were carried out with due regard to the need to eliminate unlawful racial discrimination and to promote equality of opportunity, and good relations, between persons of different racial groups (section 71). In line with a recommendation from the Central Policy Review Staff, the government closed down both the Race Relations Board and the Community Relations Commission, creating under the act a new body responsible both for the enforcement of the law against racial discrimination and for the organization of activities designed to improve relations between persons of different racial groups. The new body was named the Commission for Racial Equality and some of the local councils changed their names accordingly. The Home Secretary recognized that, because of the word's biological connotations, there were objections to using 'racial' in this way. The legislation was nevertheless designed to counter the mistaken beliefs and actions of ordinary men and women for whom the popular understanding of race, along with colour and national origins, had become a basis for invidious distinctions. He believed that the balance of advantage lay in facing this squarely by talking of race relations and racial discrimination.

There was much discussion at the time whether it was right to amalgamate the RRB and the CRC to create a CRE. The Board thought that the functions of enforcing the law and promoting good relations were best kept separate. Mark Bonham Carter (who resigned his post with the CRC when the decision was reached) considered that the arguments were very evenly balanced (*The Observer*, 20 December 1981). The advantages of amalgamation were simply that the lessons learned by enforcing the law should be more widely diffused with local councils feeding back local experience to the central enforcement division of the commission. The danger was that the actions of community relations councils, as voluntary bodies maintained by committed people who are necessarily activists, would call in question the objectivity and impartiality of the law enforcement division which must at all times be protected. The Race Relations Board thought this danger so great as to outweigh the contrary arguments. What surely is now beyond discussion is that the best way of amalgamating the two bodies was not to close them both down and then create a new one with all the troubles that such a process entails. The new commission got off to a very bad start. Since there was so strong a case for making law enforcement its main function it would have been better to have kept the Race Relations Board, with a new name and increased funds, allowing it to take on the new additional functions as quickly as it could. A gradual expansion would have enabled it to keep to a firm structure of priorities; it could have refused to take on new responsibilities until it was ready. The CRE tried to gallop in too many directions simultaneously, so that it repeated all the organizational errors, confusion, disappointment and bitterness of the CRC and NCCI before it.

Another innovation at the same period was the establishment of what is now the Home Secretary's Advisory Council. Since it exists to advise the minister, any work it may do would attract little publicity, but it would appear to have been inactive and the parliamentary Home Affairs Committee in its 1980–1 Report on Racial Disadvantage (para. 38) curtly dismissed it as 'ineffective'.

The Labour government did not in any significant manner change the immigration policy prevailing before 1974. This policy was sympathetic towards the reunification of families by permitting the dependents of New Commonwealth immigrants in Britain to join the family bread-winner. Changes in detail have occurred concerning the granting of entry permits to people overseas who have just married or wish to marry people who are residents, but the overall pattern has been one of restricting immigration. In 1976–7 the parliamentary Select Committee noted that the character of West Indian migration had changed so that there was a net overflow from the United Kingdom of persons of West

Indian origin. In 1981–2 the Home Affairs Committee reported to parliament that primary immigration from the Indian Sub-Continent (i.e. the immigration of persons with work permits as opposed to their dependents) had declined, only 627 permits having been issued in 1980. Few cases remained of people entitled to remain because they had been 'ordinarily resident' in the United Kingdom on 1 January 1973. The wives of men who had entered the United Kingdom after that date continued to be allowed to settle; they totalled 8,040 in 1981. The overall trend was one strongly in decline and would fall sharply once the queues were cleared. After the general election of 1979 and the victory of the Conservative Party, all select committees were wound up and reconstituted as committees for reviewing policies within the major fields of administration, such as home affairs and the environment. The Home Affairs committee has issued a series of reports prepared by its Sub-Committee on Race Relations and Immigration. They include:

1980–1   Racial Disadvantage
1981–2   The Commission for Racial Equality
1981–2   Immigration from the Indian Sub-Continent
1982–3   Ethnic and Racial Questions in the Census

Their decision to investigate racial disadvantage was important as marking a step forward from the consideration of policies tied to the prevention of racial discrimination. The new wording indicates an understanding that members of racial minorities may be at a disadvantage for reasons other than those of discrimination by majority members. For example, children who grow up in one-parent homes will, as a category, be at a disadvantage compared with those who grow up in two-parent homes; children whose parents cannot speak English fluently and do not understand the institutions of English society which influence children's lives will probably be at a disadvantage in school even if teachers try to help them. Gypsy children are often at a disadvantage, partly because of the hostility shown towards gypsies by people in localities in which they want to stay, but partly also because the gypsies' own previous conduct has seemed to justify suspicion of them. The rights and wrongs of gypsies can be debated, but their disadvantage is beyond dispute.

The committee declared:

> There is no inherent disadvantage in being black or brown. That cannot be stated too often or too loudly. The factors other than discrimination which can cause disadvantage arise primarily from the newness to British society of many ethnic minority groups, and from

their linguistic and cultural difference to the rest of the population . . .
many Asians have religious beliefs which can have major implications
for their economic and social existence and which can hinder their
integration in existing employment and educational patterns. But in
none of these cases does disadvantage arise from the fact of being
black or being a Moslem; white English-speaking Protestants might
find many similar disadvantages were they to settle in West Indian or
Asian countries.

The committee concentrated its attention upon four cities: Bristol,
Liverpool, Manchester and Leicester. It examined witnesses from those
central government departments most closely concerned with racial
disadvantage 'to discover both their awareness of racial disadvantage
and the extent to which it had affected their formulation and administration of policy'. They invited detailed written evidence on the employment
practices of major retailers and nationalized industries, on teacher
training, and on the use made by certain local authorities of grants under
Section 11 of the Local Government Act 1966. They published 1,290
pages of this evidence.

In its report, the committee lamented that despite the volume of
information it was 'impossible to discover the simple factual truth about
some of the most significant and apparently straightforward matters';
for example, 'we know neither the total ethnic minority population nor
their true rate of unemployment'. But since there could be no doubt that
there was 'a disturbing pattern of racial disadvantage', the committee
felt able to concentrate upon recommending measures for redressing it.

The committee was perturbed to learn from the Minister of State that
the Home Office would not call themselves a coordinating department,
but rather one 'which tries to have an over-view of the whole area of race
relations policy'. They were not satisfied with this and proposed means
for more effective policy-making. They recommended that several
government departments create specialized units for combatting racial
disadvantage. There was a need for policy-relevant social research.
Section 11 and Urban Programme grants should be continued but the
administration of these programmes should be improved in particular
respects. Local authorities should review their arrangements for
consultation with ethnic minorities. They should monitor the services
they provided. The committee made further recommendations (to a total
of fifty-seven) about the allocation of council houses, day-care facilities
for children under five, provisions for the elderly, etc.

The committee noted that a number of employers, particularly large
ones, had declared themselves equal opportunity employers. Others had

held back. One of the stronger fears was the belief that this was the first step towards the sort of reverse discrimination and quota enforcement practiced in the United States. The committee listed the various grounds on which employers and trade unionists opposed proposals for ethnic monitoring. They did not lend their support to the CRE's draft code of practice (which had not then been put before parliament). They reported that British Airways would welcome 'firm and clear guidelines from Government that the form of categorization proposed by the Commission and its utilization by the Civil Service and nationalized industries is acceptable'. British Airways were understandably concerned as to 'the Government's commitment to either the principle or form of monitoring proposed by the Commission'. The committee expressed its approval of equal opportunity employment declarations, and recommended ethnic monitoring, to include the civil service; it strongly recommended that whether or not monitoring was introduced employers and employees should together work out means for eradicating discrimination.

The introduction of ethnic monitoring in the civil service was seen by the committee as an earnest of the government's commitment to the more general declarations of ministerial speeches. Ministers had told the civil service unions in 1976 that further action was necessary. A study by an independent body of the procedures and of possible hazards in them, had described some possible methods of monitoring. A joint working party representing employers and unions had been meeting. The employers wanted a national census of civil servants in which employers would record their own ethnicity, to be followed up by some form of monitoring. The non-industrial unions were sympathetic towards this, the industrial unions opposed. In oral evidence MPs were sharply critical of all parties for their failure to make more rapid progress.

In their reply to the committee, the government accepted the general intent of the report while adding that an overriding objective was the creation of a stronger and more prosperous economy. They had reexamined official procedures in many areas in the light of the committee's comments, but they were unwilling to establish specialist units concerned with racial disadvantage in the various departments. On the key question of employment, however, they said no more than that 'Effective action to ensure equality of treatment and opportunity in the workplace can only be achieved if all those concerned work for it together and the code of practice prepared by the Commission for Racial

Equality covers the responsibilities of employers, individual employees, trade unions and employment agencies.' This was a clear refusal to show the sort of commitment for which British Airways, and doubtless other employers, had been looking.

Since the presentation of the report in 1981 there has been significant progress in the monitoring of equal opportunity within the civil service. Studies have started in several areas. Some of the credit for this is due to the Home Affairs Committee's pressure. One of the difficulties all along, however, has been that of the mode of classification to be used when assigning people to one ethnic group or another. To illustrate this it is convenient to interrupt the chronological sequence of the committee's reports and quote some of the evidence they received in their wide-ranging 1982–3 enquiry into Ethnic and Racial Questions in the Census. When Professor Robert Moore and Dr Adam Vetta's testimony was examined, the latter, referring to the Office of Population Censuses and Surveys, said

> The OPCS people expect me to describe myself as 'Indian'. I cannot, because I am no longer Indian. They also have the concept of a mixed race. They want my children to describe themselves as of mixed race; rightly they regard themselves as being English, their mother is English, they were born in England. My children do not know any Indian language, the only language they know is English. They are very well adapted to the English conditions, and they know more about English traditions than I do . . . How dare anyone suggest that they should describe themselves as of mixed race?

To which Professor Moore added:

> Much more is to be gained from asserting that people like his children are British than is to be gained by forcing them into describing themselves in certain ways in which they may not have normally thought of themselves . . . Would you expect parents to define the ethnicity of their children?

Most of the social scientists who testified to this point insisted that ethnicity was not an objective classification but something subjective and dependent upon social context. For example, two outstanding sportsmen of dark complexion had refused to be included in a book about black sportsmen, one on the grounds that he had an English mother and thought this would be an insult to her, the other, who had been fostered in a rural area by another white parent, insisted 'I may be black but this is not the most important thing about me.' Several witnesses thought that one source of the difficulty lay in the way being

English and being white were equated. Dr Vetta said his children 'would call themselves English, and "English" does not really mean they have to be white'.

The committee was caught between two principles. On the one hand it was told by the Institute of Personnel Management that any government decision not to include in the census any question on ethnic origin would discourage employers from systematic recording of such information. The government must set an example and the census was an important place in which to do so. On the other hand, MPs could see that it was undesirable to reinforce ethnic division by giving official sanction to a set of categories which made it difficult for children not entirely of English origin to think of themselves as English. To overcome the fearful heritage of mistaken theories about race, it was necessary to weaken racial categories and look to the pattern of Brazil rather than that of the United States. The MPs placed more weight on the former principle because they accepted a degree of inaccuracy in any statistics based on self-assignment. Mr Alex Lyon told a Jewish spokesman: 'If 3 per cent of Jews or people of Jewish ancestry say they are not Jews it does not make a lot of difference to the total picture . . . What you are looking for are the people who assess themselves as minorities and are treated as minorities in a way that is to their disadvantage.' So the committee opted for an ethnic question, one which they said would 'be anathema to many social scientists' (and which did indeed include the objectionable category 'mixed race'). Equally important, perhaps, was their criticism of some unnamed government departments. The OPCS had run into difficulty in Haringey (North London) when they tested a possible form of ethnic question for the 1981 census. This was partly because the Registrar-General was unable to explain for what purpose government departments wanted the information. He was unable to do so because these departments could not tell him. The committee was surprised how little serious thought they appeared to have given to the value of a census in delineating racial disadvantage. Often they had only the vaguest idea how other questions in the census might be used in giving extra weight to ethnic data. They found the Treasury's indifference quite extraordinary. Maximal utilization of available data by central and local government departments, and by ethnic minority groups, were vital elements in the policy process.

Public awareness of the need to monitor equal opportunity policies was doubtless heightened by the riots of 1980 and 1981. The first occurred on 2 April 1980 in an area of central Bristol with a substantial black resident population. A group of black youngsters started to stone a squad of police officers who had raided a cafe for the illegal possession and sale of alcoholic drink. The disorder spread with crowds of young people, white and black but predominantly young, attacking the police all evening. Eventually the police withdrew from the area for several hours and there was some looting of shops. In April to July of the following year there was a series of urban riots in areas of black and Asian settlement: Southall, Brixton, Toxteth (Liverpool), Moss Side (Manchester), Chapeltown (Leeds), Highfields (Leicester), the West Midlands and elsewhere. These were the subject of an enquiry by Lord Scarman who found them to be communal disorders with a strong racial element. The riots attracted intense publicity at home and overseas, evoking a national sense of shock. The images conveyed by the mass media over-dramatized the events; they underplayed white involvement (of over 4,000 persons arrested in the July riots, 70 per cent were white) and they failed to make connections with other forms of public violence. Many of the youngsters who crowded the streets will have been there to see the fun, and many will have welcomed the opportunity to have a go at the police. As a form of entertainment, rioting could be compared with the excitement young men derive from the prospect of fighting between supporters of rival football teams: they demonstrate their manliness and threaten physical attacks that only occasionally take place. Moreover it was only later in the year that a Home Office study provided a measure of the violence directed against individual members of the racial minorities. It showed the incidence of racial attacks on Asians to be fifty times greater, and that on blacks over thirty-six times greater, than upon white people. The Home Secretary acknowledged that such attacks were more common than his advisers had realized, that they seemed to be on the increase, and that a new response was necessary. Bengali-speaking people from Bangladesh who have settled in East London were particularly subject to racial attack and they had complained of police indifference. The attacks did not appear to be orchestrated by extremist organizations, a conclusion that makes the evidence the more frightening.

The British riots of 1980 and 1981, like most riots, were very complex events. As Stan Taylor (in Benyon, 1984: 20–34) has shown, different facets of them can be explained more or less satisfactorily by the theories of sociology (functionalist or conflictual), social psychology (cognitive or Freudian), economic (rational choice), political science (conspiracy, institutional failure, bargaining, or response to repression), or in terms of contagion (geographical, media, or tradition). Anyone who seeks to bring partial explanations together in a comprehensive account selects certain aspects as more deserving of attention and his or her political outlook will influence this situation more than it would in a limited analysis within the framework of a particular social science. A comprehensive account has also to be historical and, since its success is weighed against more subjective criteria, it may be distinguished as an interpretation rather than an explanation. When constructing an interpretation of riots such as those of 1981, a conservative is likely to presuppose that since the institutions of British society were adequate to advance the interests of deprived groups, the rioting must be attributed to a mixture of conspiratorial motives, desire for gain or entertainment, irrational impulses, and imitation. A liberal will assume that the institutions of British society require reform and a radical that they are due for fundamental change; their interpretations and prescriptions will embody different mixes of the factors separately covered by the various social-science theories.

Someone who seeks a comprehensive interpretation (and Chapter 1 has emphasized that every scholar operates with some set of assumptions as to what is most important) is not free to disregard inconvenient evidence. For example, there is good reason to believe that in many inner city neighbourhoods police officers had behaved in an excessively heavy-handed way towards young men seen on the streets, and particularly towards black youths. It is quite implausible to deny that police practices prior to 1981 could have been better and that had they been so the likelihood of rioting would have been lessened. Nor is it sensible to reject any association between rioting and social deprivation or to deny that the riots had a political dimension on the grounds that the rioters may not have thought of their actions as political. On the other hand it stretches the evidence too far to picture the disturbances as the revolt of whole black communities. The police and the rioters responded to each other's behaviour and justified their own actions as responses to what the others had done. To talk of revolt is to imply an opposition to fundamental features of the social order whereas such research as has been carried out suggests that young blacks who live in London in the circumstances of greatest disadvantage have positive feelings towards those fundamental features. They may feel the more frustrated because they do not reject the society but seek only changes that will enable them to fulfil their aspirations by participating in it (Gaskell and Smith, 1981).

The climate of white public opinion in late 1981 was decidedly different from that which prevailed in 1967. Maybe the positive and negative reactions to the riots cancelled each other out, and the reasons for the change should be sought in the 1970s. Nor is it easy to pin down the nature of the difference, and there is a danger that any commentator will attribute to other people the sorts of change in outlook that he or she has undergone. Anyone who attempts to detect what has changed has necessarily to pay most attention to opinion amongst the white majority and particularly to that articulate minority which has most influence upon the mass media. In 1967 there was an acceptance that the problem of integrating the immigrants was a problem on the social level which could be solved by the appropriate policy changes and in particular by taking action to help the immigrants. It was based on an over-optimistic conception of the nature of 'the problem' and it over-estimated the speed at which the remedial measures would take effect. It under-estimated the extent to which members of the majority would have to change their customary ways.

Members of the general public who in 1967 accepted that it was right that things should be done for the immigrants were, in effect, told in the following years that this was the wrong attitude. It was patronizing: minority members should be allowed to do things for themselves and their fellows. Moreover, the things that were being done for the immigrants were insufficient; more far-reaching changes were necessary. These desired changes were described only in general terms. No detailed and practicable proposals were advanced and there were no minority leaders able to negotiate on behalf of their groups. The conflict between the rhetoric and the reality caused some sympathetic people to lose interest. Many people who were once willing to work for community relations agencies have withdrawn in frustration and a similar withdrawal seems to have occurred in public opinion. It has been the greater because public expectations have been unrealistically high and those concerned to promote racial harmony have too often despised modest programmes directed towards limited objectives – but programmes with some chance of success. For this the Commission for Racial Equality is in part responsible.

In the 1981–2 session of parliament the Home Affairs Committee investigated the commission and was scathing in its judgements. They undertook the investigation because the MPs were 'not greatly impressed by the quality of the evidence submitted by the CRE' to their inquiry into racial disadvantage. Apart from their own misgivings there was 'widespread public criticism' of the commission. On this occasion they did not cast their net as widely as for previous enquiries, choosing to take evidence only from the commission itself, trade unions to which its staff belonged, the National Association of Community Relations Councils, and the Home Office. The sentiments of some of the five MPs who formed the sub-committee were soon apparent. Mr George Gardiner (Conservative MP for Reigate) addressed Mr David Lane, a former Conservative MP and Home Office minister who was chairman of the CRE:

> We noted particularly after a riot in Bristol the lecture which you delivered to society at large drawing very speedily conclusions from the situation there, and there have been other occasions since when you will acknowledge you have very quickly made public statements. I would have thought, or I put it to you, that that is a role which is not very easily reconciled with the role of a law enforcement agency commanding broad public support?

Mr Alex Lyon (Labour MP for York) could scarcely conceal his contempt for the CRE's record as a law enforcement agency: 'We gave you the biggest powers in the Western world in relation to law enforcement. What have you done with them?' Mr John Hunt (Conservative MP for Bromley, Ravensbourne) asked if the representatives of the CRE would 'Acknowledge that in some parts of the country there are grave doubts and apprehensions about some of the activities of some of the CRCs and CROs?' and elicited agreement. The MPs were critical of what seemed like an indiscriminate distribution of grants. Mr Gardiner accused them of acting like 'a sort of coloured sports council' and wondered, for example, why a body called Housewives in Dialogue should be supported to the tune of £950. Mr Lyon recalled: 'I once went to a Sikh temple in Leeds, where they were asking me for a grant from urban aid in order that they could improve their Sikh temple and they all drove up in Mercedes motor cars in order to ask me for the money.' Nor was the National Association of Community Relations Councils any more complimentary towards the CRE, referring to 'its current failure', its 'overall lack of coherence in policy formation, combined with a failure to integrate the different functional elements in the pursuit of specified objectives; confusion about the nature of its relationship with independent organizations [the CRC] . . .', and 'its lack of professional competence' which, allegedly, included the failure to abide by its promises and even to keep proper minutes or answer correspondence.

Thus, the Home Affairs Committee did not lack support for its own conclusions when it reported to parliament that the CRE's gravest defect was incoherence. 'The Commission operate without any obvious sense of priorities or any clearly defined objectives. There are few subjects on which they prove unwilling to pronounce and few projects on which they are unwilling to embark. Where specific policy objectives have been established, they are rarely translated into concrete activity ... A distressing amount of energy is frittered away.' The committee criticized the commission for acting as if it were a 'shadow race relations department' of government and for failing to appreciate that the task of promoting good race relations lies mainly with the institutions of central and local government. 'Only they have the power and resources to make the necessary impact. The pretence that a small statutory body can undertake that task assumes a responsibility it cannot discharge and the attempt can only lead to frustration among the staff and disillusionment amongst the black minority.' The committee criticized what they saw as the commission's tendency 'to adopt the role of spokesman for what they interpret as the views of ethnic minorities, and to prefer this role to their true one of a quasi-judicial statutory Commission'. Their management was 'weak'; staff morale was 'not high'; professionalism was 'a quality which is not at present greatly in evidence'. Referring to the local community relations councils as CRCs, the committee reported with asperity that 'The amount of energy which is thus wasted on conflict is appalling. CRCs trying to get rid of their CROs; CROs losing their jobs when the Commission withdrew support from a CRC; junior CROs undermining their superiors – these and other tales retailed in evidence to the Select Committee give cause for concern that the effectiveness of local relations work is being severely undermined by an atmosphere of bickering and backbiting.' In a series of places there had been debilitating troubles, Islington, Newham, Brent, Crawley, Oxford and Wolverhampton among them.

The committee recommended that the commission should continue to have the two functions of enforcing the law and promoting good race relations, but advised that their promotional work should be restricted to that which was dictated by the need to eradicate racial discrimination. They were alarmed that such a high proportion of the commission's resources was used for other purposes and dismayed that the commission had so little to show for its work in the enforcement field. Of the commission's 224 members of staff fifty-three were employed in the equal opportunities division (the one concerned with enforcement) and only four members of the staff were legally qualified. In a period of four years the commission had undertaken forty-five strategic reviews of organizations suspected of doing insufficient to promote equality of opportunity. Only ten of these reviews had been completed, mostly into small organizations, and some of these ten were hangovers from reviews commenced by the Race Relations Board. The committee was dissatisfied with the use by the CRE of local community relations councils in this field. The community relations councils could have developed a capacity to take over much of the work on complaints of racial discrimination but the commission had failed to promote such a transfer. The committee looked forward to increased action by local authorities to take over tasks presently performed by CROs. As this transfer took place financial support for the CRE could be reduced proportionately.

The government accepted many of the committee's recommendations but it did not agree that the commission's promotional and educational work could be as narrowly confined as the committee envisaged. Nor was the government aware of any dramatic growth in the readiness of local authorities themselves to make special staffing provisions for race relations work.

It was suggested in the press that the Home Affairs Committee's criticisms of the CRE were partizan, reflecting the hostility of some committee members towards the commission and what it stood for. The report was also criticized for failing to analyze the shortcomings of the present government and its predecessor. The last chairmen of the Race Relations Board (Sir Geoffrey Wilson) and the Community Relations Commission (Mark Bonham Carter) both emphasized this, while the latter regretted that the committee had not properly considered the relationship between the commission and the community relations councils. It is to these councils that the next chapter turns.

6

Community relations councils

The first research worker to interview members of a sample of local councils concluded that some of the quite considerable variation in their character could be traced to their particular histories (Abbott, 1971: 344). Who had started them, and for what purpose, could be important. Among the first was a Committee for the Welfare of Colonial Workers in Bristol founded in 1951–2 by the social and industrial adviser to the bishop. Its membership tells its own story about majority–minority relations at the time for it included representatives from the Co-operative Society, the Council of Social Service, the Council of Churches, the Chamber of Commerce, the Immigration Department of the Home Office, Her Majesty's Prisons, the National Assistance Board, and the Society of Friends. Sometime in the 1960s it became the Coordinating Committee concerned with race relations and immigrants. It met with a leading Methodist minister as chairman and its members included representatives of the Baptist Mills Group of Schools, Bristol College of Science and Technology, Bristol Constabulary, Bristol Corporation (Departments of Education and Public Health), Bristol Council of Christian Churches, Bristol Council of Social Service, Bristol Trades Council, Bristol West Indian Association, Bristol University Student Christian Movement, Bristol Youth Council and West Indian Development Council, City Council and Citizen Party, City Council Labour Party, Co-operative Retail Society, Dockland Settlement, Italian Consulate, Methodist Churches, Ministry of Labour (Bristol Employment Exchange), National Society for the Prevention of Cruelty to Children, two Anglican churches, the Society of Friends, the West Indian Nationalist Society and the YMCA. In 1967 a voluntary liaison committee (called the Bristol Community Council) was established and the coordinating committee wound up.

If a local committee was recognized by the National Committee for Commonwealth Immigrants the latter body made a grant towards the salary of a full-time official. It expected the local authority to provide an office and basic services for the benefit of that official. In its notes about the formation of such committees (reprinted in Patterson, 1969: 431–4) the main prerequisites for recognition are listed as: (i) The sponsorship of the mayor and the interest of the local authority; (ii) Full participation by the whole community, both host and immigrant; (iii) A widely representative basis, non-political and non-sectarian, and embracing both voluntary and statutory organization. 'It should be emphasized at every stage that this is not a committee to serve the interests of one section of the community, but a committee to promote racial harmony. It is therefore beneficial to all.' The creation, by the NCCI of a network of such committees throughout the country was a significant achievement. If discrimination was to be reduced, and good relations promoted, a first priority was to win the support of the local authorities. Little could be achieved without them. Many must have regarded the question of community relations as constituting at most a peripheral problem, and have believed that their existing structure, supplemented by the voluntary agencies, was quite sufficient.

The committees varied in the way they went about their work. Dipak Nandy wrote in 1967 (quoted by Hill and Issacharoff, 1971: 29) that

> Voluntary Liaison Committees have always had a choice, one which has been masked by the imprecision of the concept of liaison (for it suggests a symmetrical, two way relationship which does not obtain in real life). The choice is between interpreting the demands for equal opportunities of the minority to the dominant white society and, on the other hand, acting as the spokesman of that society to the minority group. In effect, the V.L.C.s have uniformly chosen the second alternative.

Hannan Rose described the same opposition in slightly different terms when reporting on his interviews with members of these committees. He identified one view, which he called 'radical', for it contended that the committee should lead the disadvantaged – immigrants and others – to becoming full citizens and should seek to influence the whole community by explaining what had to be done to reduce racial tension. To this was opposed a 'conservative view' that the committee should complement existing institutions, help the immigrants conform to local expectations, and refrain from comments on controversial topics lest this interfere with the committee's other objectives (Abbott, 1971: 343). Both these viewpoints were reasonable. What took time was for people with different views to learn to recognize the sort of tasks on which committees could take action with a good chance of success, and how to conduct their internal discussions. Representatives of the majority had a lot to learn about minority members and indeed about their own unexamined assumptions concerning, and attitudes towards, the immigrants. Representatives of the minorities had a lot to learn about the institutions of government and administration. It was only to be expected that there would be a period of adjustment (which to many participants would appear as a period of frustration) in which the councils established working relations and identified their options.

A vital element in the new structure was the full-time official who serviced the committee and played a most important part in the implementation of whatever policy it decided upon. The officials were asked to do more than ordinary mortals could manage, and a series of interviews in 1968 found the mood that prevailed amongst them to be one of qualified pessimism (Abbott, 1971: 382). According to *Colour and Citizenship* (Rose, 1969: 728) 'The pivot of the system is the paid liaison officer.' He had to serve many masters, being employed by the Liaison Committee, whereas his salary came from the NCCI which had to be satisfied about his competence and which assisted the local body in recruiting and training him. The NCCI, if dissatisfied, could withdraw its grant. Since local authority support was also required, the official had to work closely with local officialdom and often became identified with them. In *Colour and Citizenship* it was suggested that it would be better if a corps of liaison officers were recruited and trained by the Community Relations Commission, then seconded to serve the local committees or councils. That proposal was not adopted. The number of paid officials grew substantially: by 1969 there were seventy-eight community relations councils with forty-two full-time officers; in 1980 104 community relations councils had 226 professional staff funded by the CRE while 170 were funded by local authorities and 119 from other sources including the Manpower Services Commission and the Urban Programme. Despite this increase, despite the dissatisfaction voiced by the officers, despite the great strains which the structure generated (and which were increased when a system of annual reporting was introduced), and despite a series of working parties established by the CRC and the CRE to review the position, the initial solution has not been superseded, presumably because all the alternatives seemed even less attractive. The creation of a centrally employed corps of liaison officers could have been seen as an invitation to local authorities to diminish their support. A purely local system would have permitted too much variation, a lack of coordination and in some places inactivity. The involvement of local people in a voluntary capacity had many drawbacks but without these people there would have been insufficient pressure. To make an impact it was necessary to cultivate as many allies as possible by drawing in a wide range of organizations.

When the NCCI was transformed into the Community Relations Commission many of the local bodies followed suit by changing their names. The Bristol one became the Bristol Community Relations Council. Its objectives were declared to be:

 (i) to advance the education of the inhabitants of the city and county of Bristol without distinction of sex or race or of political, religious or other opinions and to provide facilities in the interests of social welfare for recreation and leisure time occupation with the object of improving the conditions of life of the said inhabitants;

 (ii) to promote and organize cooperation in the achievement of the above purposes and to that end bring together in council representatives of the statutory authorities and voluntary organizations engaged in the furtherance of the above purposes within the said city and county;

(iii) in furtherance of the above purpose (but not otherwise) to advance the education of the inhabitants concerning good citizenship in a multi-racial society and the intellectual, artistic, economic and cultural backgrounds of the inhabitants of the said city and county. The council shall be non-party in politics and non-sectarian in religion.

The legal phraseology was of little assistance so long as the objectives were defined so widely. Soon afterwards the council was invited to join other organizations in expressing opposition to a projected South African cricket tour on the ground that the team had been selected according to race. To have such a team visit Bristol was said to be bad for community relations in Bristol so that it fell within the terms of the council's objectives for it to express such opposition: it did so, unanimously. It might have been better for the organizers of the opposition to try to secure the support of the city council and other major institutions of the locality. To identify a relatively weak body like the community relations council with a movement perceived by some whites as threatening their enjoyment of sport weakened the community relations council to some extent, yet once the issue of principle was raised, members of the council felt obliged to vote for it; there was a parallel with the position of Sikhs in Wolverhampton who felt obliged to support the turban activists even though they doubted the wisdom of the campaign.

To start with, black West Indians, mostly from Jamaica, were the most numerous ethnic minority in Bristol, but during the 1970s the number of Asians increased and the first person from an ethnic minority to become chairman of what was by then the Bristol Council for Racial Equality, in 1982, was a Sikh. In some towns the character of the community relations councils has depended very much upon the relative size of the different minorities and the extent to which their representatives saw themselves as sent to struggle on behalf of their own groups in a contest for prestige.

The conditions under which this sort of communalism is to be expected were illuminated by F. G. Bailey (1965: 9–12), in a study of Indian village politics which is highly relevant to any understanding of the variations between these councils in Britain. Bailey's attention was drawn by policies instituted in some Indian states to reward those villages where the Sarpanch (or chairman) of the Panchayat (or council) and at least 80 per cent of the members were elected unopposed, and by the argument of such people as J. P. Narayan that it was better for members of a community to reach a decision by consensus than by voting. He noted that some councils tried more resolutely than others to reach decisions by consensus, and that some were more successful in their attempts. What distinguished the one kind of council from the other? Size was clearly important, for 'a decision by consensus cannot be reached in a council where *active* members number more than about fifteen' but among the smaller councils the crucial factor was the relationship between a council member and the people he represented. This led Bailey to distinguish between elite councils and arena councils:

> Elite councils are those which are, or consider themselves to be (whether they admit it openly or not), a ruling oligarchy. The dominant cleavage in such a group is between the elite council (including, where appropriate, the minority from which it is recruited) and the public; that is to say, the dominant cleavage is horizontal. The opposite kind of council is the arena council. These exist in groups in which the dominant cleavages are vertical. The council is not so much a corporate body with interests against its public, but an arena in which the representatives of segments in the public come into conflict with one another.

What Bailey calls a cleavage can be seen as a boundary between two networks of bargaining relations. Where there is an arena council the members are involved in bargaining with their supporters but not with other members belonging to other parties. Where there is an elite council members bargain with their supporters to obtain election but, once elected, concentrate upon bargaining inside the council and support one another in resisting pressure from the electors to reopen bargaining with them before the next election campaign starts. However, such a view deals only with the positive aspects of bargaining with promises to trade services, and not with the exchange of threats. In political and industrial disputes one party may declare its intention of disrupting or terminating the whole set of relations which give rise to the dispute if the other party fails to make concessions. Bargaining about threats is characteristic of arena councils and can be seen as a consequence of the parties' inability to engage in positive bargaining. If a cleavage is to be seen as a boundary it is therefore one across which there may be negative bargaining concerning actions which may reduce the welfare of people on both sides. The less power a bargainer has over those whom he represents, the more he is likely to engage in negative bargaining; though he has little scope to make promises on behalf of those he represents, he can forecast that unless their expectations are met they will take disruptive action in spite of any advice from him to the contrary.

Since many members of the Asian minorities are accustomed to a zero-sum pattern of bargaining with other minorities, caste against caste, Sikh against Hindu, Moslem against Sikh, and so on, it would not be surprising if this did not contribute to the establishment of arena-style community relations councils in Britain. The council provided an arena in which they could compete for *izzat*. Some Asian representatives in particular have thought it their duty as members of a community relations council to work on behalf of their own particular minority. Where one group has been dominant, council members from other groups have felt entitled to repudiate policies they had formally accepted since they saw no benefit in expressing open opposition. One Moslem leader complained to community relations councils head-quarters that a case of discrimination had occurred in the giving of planning permission: it transpired that one group were being allowed to build a mosque with a minaret two feet higher than that of a rival mosque. Such attitudes are not limited to Asians (or to minorities for that matter). A study of community relations councils (Barker, 1975: 11) described the success of one council which obtained a grant to open a hostel for Asian girls who felt unable to live with their families: 'West Indians tend to resent this award when some of their boys also badly need a hostel and they asked first.' The incident reveals another aspect of a community relations council's difficulties when it goes on to say: 'Some Asian parents, however, are also angry at the grant: "You are trying to steal our daughters from us". One local social services professional observes that some Asian parents simply refuse to recognize the fact that some Asian girls become pregnant and that they are made so by Asian boys.' The council hoped that the hostel would eventually become multi-racial.

Community relations councils are also divided along a dimension that cuts across ethnic differences. A common pattern has been for there to be a council with over 100 members meeting four or five times a year, and a smaller executive, probably of less than twenty people meeting more frequently to conduct much of the business. At council meetings much might depend on which members attended, spoke, or stayed for any vote. These meetings provided an audience for the orators. Though the paid officials were, according to the constitution, employed by the council, it was virtually to the executive and its chairman that they were in practice accountable. Though the council, as a whole stood in a staff relationship to the division of the local authority whose activities they sought to influence, the executive functioned best if it stood in a line relationship to the officers and the council. It was responsible in practice for the way in which the council's scarce resources were utilized. If its policies were not to be upset at council meetings the members of the executive had to bargain amongst themselves and reach decisions which they could all support when they were reported to the council.

Inevitably there were differences in the motivations of the members of the community relations council who belonged to the racial majority and those from the minorities. Minority members were there because they and those with whom they identified suffered from ignorance and prejudice on the part of the people belonging to the majority. Majority members joined such councils, usually, for more altruistic reasons. In the early years the churches often took the lead. Then more people were drawn in who as teachers, lawyers and as local councillors had come to perceive community relations as important. The whites, if they felt frustrated by the failure of the community relations council to meet their expectations, always had somewhere else to go. They could put their energies into some other organization which offered them a similar opportunity to work for their objectives. The minority people did not have the same opportunity for exit because there were fewer alternative organizational avenues for them. If they felt frustrated they were less likely to leave. There was a danger that the white people who supported such councils would become quite unrepresentative of white opinion in general and therefore that there would not be full participation by the whole community in the work of the community relations council.

After 1968 a new kind of argument was heard. It was based on a philosophy of society that may be called radical and distinguished from the conservative and liberal philosophies mentioned in Chapter 3. The radical view was manifested in the first two reviews of community relations councils: a comparative study of eight councils carried out in 1968–9 by Michael J. Hill and Ruth M. Issacharoff (1971) and a comparison of the position of black urban immigrants in United States and British cities by Ira Katznelson (1973) which included an examination of the council in Nottingham. Three characteristics of the views of these authors and others of similar orientation were:

(i)   ethnic relations in British cities need to be seen in terms of the position of black people throughout the world and of the British colonial legacy;

(ii) the politics of immigration in Britain in the 1950s and 1960s were, at root, the politics of race;

(iii) racial polarization is the best stimulus to progressive change in this field.

These propositions may be contrasted with three which identify the liberal philosophy (and to which some Conservative Party members subscribed):

(i)   policy should be pragmatic, trying to solve small-scale problems as they arose at the local level;

(ii) white racial sentiment is fluid; more favourable attitudes can be cultivated by low pressure tactics;

(iii) it is best to cater to individual needs, allowing minority people to move into the majority society.

The third, conservative, view was less well articulated. Its core was the resigned acceptance that:

(i)   the immigrants could not be persuaded to go back and could not be forcibly repatriated;

(ii) therefore it was best to minimize the damage that had been caused to the social fabric. The law of the land must be enforced in an even-handed manner and individual welfare must be safeguarded;

(iii) yet it was not to be expected that there would be very much racial mixing.

The radicals derived their inspiration from the success of the black consciousness movement in the United States in the mid-1960s and from the almost simultaneous rise of academic interest in Marxism. The influence of the United States can be seen in many fields, not least in the adoption of the expression 'black' as a substitution for the previous 'coloured' without any consideration of whether the people to be designated by it on the eastern side of the Atlantic corresponded with those on the western side. Katznelson (1973: 33) declared:

> West Indians, Pakistanis, Indians, African blacks, and African Asians whose social, cultural, and religious differences from each other are often greater than the intrinsic differences that distinguish them from white Englishmen . . . should be considered analytically as a single group because, as a collectivity, they form a meaningful stratification unit whose members share objective interests, similar vantage points, and a shared consciousness, actual or potential.

This is typical of the dogmatism of the intellectual movement and period. It may indeed be useful to consider all non-whites as constituting a single unit for certain purposes but, if so, this is something to be demonstrated by scholarly argument. If it is useful in some ways it may not be useful for other purposes and may even be an obstacle to the kind of conceptualization some analyses require. Similar objections exist to the designation of all members of this category as black.

In the 1960s in the United States the word 'racism', which earlier had been used to designate a doctrine, dogma or ideology, was pressed into political service as an unfavourable epithet applicable to attitudes, behaviour and even whoie societies. It was an adjective with a powerful resonance: once someone was labelled as a racist he or she was placed at a great disadvantage in argument. Liberals, if they make use of a concept of racism, employ it as part of an explanation, trying to account for the attitudes or behaviour of people involved in inter-racial relations. The radicals agree that some understanding of social relations can be obtained by the positivistic methods of conventional social science, yet maintain that the only true understanding is that obtained by locating these patterns in relation to the development of the systems of which they form part; only in this way can societies be regulated for the general good. Since all social phenomena are continually changing, so the nature of racism changes and it is misconceived to try to formulate a sharp definition. The question of whether a belief, attitude or practice is, or is not, racist, is ultimately to be decided by its place in a historical sequence.

In the United States Afro-Americans were able to mobilize political strength by emphasizing the distinction between them and the whites.

They benefited from white guilt about the way in which blacks had been treated over the centuries, and were able to incorporate an element of threat in the cry for black power. In Britain the New Commonwealth minorities were divided and weak, so it was the more important to shake progressive sections of white opinion into a realization of the nature of the processes at work. In its new sense, the concept of racism could be used to this end. Previously there had been an acceptance that Britain, like every other society, had its own forms of ethnocentrism and that this was an important element in the opposition to New Commonwealth immigration. Ethnocentrism implies a continuous range of attitudes, differing in degree, so that fair-skinned English-speaking immigrants are more acceptable than dark-skinned people who do not speak English. The radicals insisted that Britain was not an ethnocentric but a racist society and that the clearest proof was to be found in the 1968 Immigration Act designed to keep out British subjects from East Africa with dark complexions, while admitting those with pale complexions.

The Marxist influence can be seen in some of the ways that trans-atlantic stimuli were transformed in their British applications, but it is particularly evident in the claim that the presence of the ethnic minorities in Britain is evidence of the working out of general laws of capitalist development. The Third World countries are first colonized and then some of their populations are drawn in to assist the ailing industries of the metropolitan powers. This process increasingly sorts out the various contending groups into the polarities of left versus right and proletariat versus bourgeoisie. Any political action which is not oriented to these trends must in the long run be exposed as diversionary. Thus in the preface to the Hill and Issacharoff study the reader is informed that one of the authors 'does not believe that the necessary comprehensive social change of a socialist kind could ever come about through the voluntary activities of a government-sponsored organiza-tion in the present society, but she hopes that there may be some value in publishing the findings as evidence of the epiphenomenal nature of the community relations movement'. Radicals, as can be seen, are pessi-mistic about the possibilities for cumulative small-scale social reform, believing that the powerful groups will always divert those reforms to ensure that their interests are not threatened. They contend that racial harmony can be attained only when racial groups can negotiate as equals and that the best prospect is for community relations councils to be controlled by the minorities and speak for them. This argument passes over the history of CARD which, once captured by the radicals, collapsed.

The liberals opposed these views at many points. They have pointed to the success of the Race Relations Acts in reducing racial discrimination, being heartened by what has been achieved as well as disappointed by how much still remains to be done. Tolerance of insulting and abusive language appears to have declined and many people who previously would not listen to any discussion of the problems now acknowledge that they have to be tackled. They reject the implication that racial attitudes conform with a left–right polarity, remarking that some attitudes, like those concerning crime, punishment and sexual morality, belong on a different dimension and that attitudes towards racial matters fit that other dimension more closely than one which primarily measures opinions about the public ownership of the means of production. They too may deplore the 1968 Commonwealth Immigration Act while observing that its effect was not so much to keep out dark-skinned British subjects as to delay their entry. Some of the differences between liberals and radicals can be mitigated, if not resolved, by evidence as to matters of fact, but other differences run deeper. Where liberals start with the individual and look up towards the social aggregate, the radicals start with historical processes and work downwards, stressing the power of aggregate trends to constrain individual behaviour. The liberal philosophy has difficulty coming to terms with ideas of group rights, group burdens and group responses. The radical philosophy is inclined to neglect the ways in which individuals refuse to fit into group moulds.

Differences of political philosophy are also associated with different assumptions about the nature of ethnicity, though the association is not always very close. Conservatives are more inclined to see ethnicity as a primordial attribute, something almost as basic to an individual's identity as being male or female, whereas liberals and many radicals see it as something circumstantial in that its whole character and expression is a product of time and place (Glazer and Moynihan, 1975: 19–20). The primordial view of ethnicity is obviously akin to the conception of history as influenced by the working out of national consciousness as discussed in Chapter 2. In the contemporary world this outlook is expressed most strongly by the Afrikaners, but Jewish intellectuals who are political liberals may also perceive their own ethnicity in comparable terms.

After the return of a Labour government in 1974 a review of the working of the 1968 Race Relations Act was undertaken. To assist in this the Runnymede Trust carried out a study of thirteen community relations councils using a sample designed to reflect the variety of local ethnic groupings, geographical locations and styles of work to which the councils themselves gave priority (Barker, 1975). They distinguished three types of council:

(i) the shelter-type assists immigrants with their problems as an interpreter, guide, information channel and adviser on rights;

(ii) the bridge-type provides a meeting place for community organizations from the minority ethnic groups and acts as a stimulator;

(iii) the platform-type sees its role as a campaigning organization, drawing public attention to the problems of racial discrimination and inner city deprivation.

Of the thirteen community relations councils five were of the shelter type, two bridge, four platform and two shelter/bridge. Three of the thirteen had among their local minorities a clear preponderance of people of Afro-Caribbean background, seven of Asian origin, while three were fairly evenly balanced. No association between the style of the community relations councils operations and its minority composition was mentioned. The research workers described the community relations councils sampled as being 'loose alliances of white voluntary service organizations, local authority interests, minority communities, police, church and other professional bodies'. They were so broadly based that there was no basis for action unless the key figures and their CRO had decided what they wanted and how to achieve it. What they did varied substantially, doubtless being influenced by considerations of expediency and individual enthusiasm. Indeed, when seven respondents in the same London borough were asked 'Why was your local CRC set up?' they gave very diverse answers, reflecting the differences in their conceptions of what the organization was for. In between the lines of the report can be found some indication of anxiety about the political context in which the councils had to operate. Minority spokesmen at this time were anxious about the influence of extremist organizations of the National Front kind; others, and this may have been more of a majority worry, were anxious about a 'backlash' reaction from white opinion if minority demands were pitched too high. The director of the Runnymede Trust summed up his impressions of the councils by writing:

> Some provide invaluable services, others tinker ineffectively with what the statutory health and welfare services ought to be doing. Some really do challenge policies and practices which they think are harmful to the cause of good race relations; others accept the local political status quo without question. Some should receive stronger support; others should not receive any backing at all.

The report recommended that the broad goal must be 'community development' among minority communities combined with 'public education' or 'awareness' of the nature of a multi-racial society among the general or dominant white community (a partial endorsement of the platform style). It favoured techniques for encouraging the minority communities to become independent and able to help themselves. The award of grants might be more selective. A national assessment programme should be undertaken so that a national policy allowing for local variations could be drawn up.

At much the same time the Select Committee undertook its own investigation of community relations councils. Of the eighty-five councils, eighty-two replied to a questionnaire sent to them. The committee reported that the performance and resources of the councils varied enormously and that therefore they had considered whether their work should be transferred to the local authorities. In their view, however, the active association of various kinds of groups in the work of the councils had made an important contribution to the improvement of race relations and therefore this should continue. They noted that the councils and their officers were overwhelmingly opposed to any such transfer, and the local authorities themselves had shown no wish to take over the work, recognizing that the councils served a necessary function and that some of their activities would not be appropriate to local government. The government accepted the Select Committee's recommendations in this connection but were unwilling to lay any statutory obligation upon local authorities to contribute to the financing of community relations staff.

In the 1976 Race Relations Act, section 71, the government placed upon local authorities a general duty 'to make appropriate arrangements with a view to securing that their various functions are carried out with due regard to the need (a) to eliminate unlawful racial discrimination; and (b) to promote equality of opportunity and good relations, between persons of different racial groups'. The CRE responded by arranging for teams of its officers to visit local authorities so that a specialist from the commission on, say, housing, could discuss with a housing specialist in the local authority what might be done to discharge this new duty. The response of some local authorities was to appoint their own staff to take responsibility so that they did not need to rely on the local community relations council. The Home Affairs Committee in its 1982 report on the CRE had predicted such a tendency and according to a report in *The Guardian* for 12 September 1983 they were being proved right. Several local authorities, both Labour- and Conservative-controlled, disliking the activities of their community relations councils, had withdrawn their grants. Many, especially in the big cities, had taken on some of the community relations councils' former tasks, appointing staff to work for equal treatment for non-whites in employment and council services. Such a development was surely one to be encouraged by the CRE if it meant that someone within the line of command in the administration would be speaking up for the priority to be given to Section 71 obligations and seeing that any person who disregarded the need for good racial relations was disciplined. Yet up to this time the CRE seemed to have no philosophy concerning the transfer of responsibilities to local authority personnel. If the local authority withdrew its grant, the commission was likely to take similar action. Even if the local authority assumed all the duties under Section 71 there still was, and is, a role for an independent watchdog organization, as many councillors, town clerks and social services directors made plain to the Runnymede research team.

One reason why some community relations councils have become unpopular with their local authorities has been that the councils often engage in symbolic politics. For example, when Mr Ronald Bell, a Conservative MP critical of New Commonwealth immigration, was made a knight, the Bristol Council for Racial Equality adopted a motion of protest. Again, when a South African MP paid a visit to Bristol sponsored by the British government to learn about community relations work in Britain, the Bristol council, on a majority vote, called on 'all the citizens of Bristol who believe in improving Race Relations to have nothing to do with him'. Their argument was that since he came from an all-white parliament ruling a country with an 80 per cent black population any association with him would give credibility and comfort to a racist regime. The MP (Dr Alex Boraine) retorted that his party 'is totally committed to a universal franchise for all South Africans, White and Black' and that the Bristol action only gave comfort to those white South Africans who maintained that there was no point in trying to talk with black representatives. It is appropriate to call such activity symbolic politics because it has only minimal influence on the major decision-making processes. It comes about because minority members feel they have insufficient opportunity to voice their feelings through the channels of British party politics and because the terms of reference of councils are, necessarily, so widely drawn that chairmen hesitate to rule that such motions fall outside the councils' objectives (as was discussed at the beginning of this chapter with reference to a projected cricket tour from South Africa).

Members of community relations councils can engage in symbolic politics only so long as other members permit this. A comparison with the Indian village councils mentioned earlier may be helpful. An Indian council of the arena type may be deadlocked and unable to make decisions, but since the various groups have to live together and there is no alternative of exit, they have to work out their problems. A British community relations council can more easily attract members who are representative of the minority groups than of the majority group since majority members hostile or cool towards the objectives of the council will not become members. As was noted earlier (Chapter 2, p. 26 and Chapter 6, p. 105) not all whites have any interest in reducing racial discrimination and few of them will have an interest as strong as that of minority members. In the previous chapter mention was made of the witness before the Home Affairs Committee who regretted the absence of an effective pressure group and was told that the minorities should create their own pressure groups: the community relations council was the forum in which they could bring that pressure to bear. If, however, the council becomes unrepresentative of the whole local society then some sections of it either cease attending or cease resisting motions that they know they cannot defeat. An atmosphere is created in which negative opinions, complaints and criticisms become the norm. Defences of established institutions and practices are scorned as unconvincing excuses. Constructive action is made more difficult.

At council meetings a struggle can sometimes be seen between the chairman and the members who want to engage in symbolic politics. If the executive committee members support one another and operate like an elite council in Bailey's terms they can exercise great influence at a council meeting, though there can be differences from one meeting to another because attendance varies and certain issues will ensure that particular interest groups put in an appearance. Sometimes, though, an executive itself takes the initiative by issuing a statement before the matter in question has been considered by the council. A recent incident in Avon can illustrate some of the complexities in the workings of a local authority and the community relations council's relationship to that authority.

In November 1982 a woman Sikh teacher assigned from the Avon County Council Multi-Cultural Education Centre to teach in a Bristol primary school was subjected to racial abuse in the staff room from a male English teacher. The teacher who had been insulted first tried to have her complaint dealt with through the education authority's internal grievance procedure, or by the National Union of Teachers (NUT); obtaining no satisfaction from them, she took her case to an industrial tribunal, bringing an action against the local education authority as the employer of the other teacher (as well as of herself). Despite its prior knowledge of the matter, the authority was unprepared for such an action as it was the first of its kind anywhere in the country. It took legal advice and hesitated for some time about whether it should defend the action. The National Union of Teachers also appeared to hesitate over its obligations to the teacher complained against. All of this made the teacher who had been abused feel as if she, who was the victim and an employee carrying out her employer's policies, was in some way the offender who had to justify herself. It certainly appeared as if the education authority's response was bureaucratic and insensitive towards one of its employees.

The authority decided not to contest the case and proceedings were dropped when the authority agreed that a regrettable incident of racial abuse had taken place. It paid the complainant £500 compensation and £150 in respect of the costs she had incurred. Disciplinary action was taken against the offending teacher by the school's governors. In September 1983, when the education authority agreed to the out-of-court settlement, the executive of the Bristol Council for Racial Equality unanimously adopted, and subsequently publicized, a resolution: 'BCRE deplores the fact that racist teachers can operate in Avon schools. However, it believes that this situation is a manifestation of deeply rooted structural racism which permeates education in Avon at every level and which we are committed to eradicate.' Their statement went on to say that the BCRE and Avon NUT had asked for a meeting with the officers of Avon Education Committee to discuss the implications of the case. When this was reported to the next meeting of the council, a local Labour councillor, who was also vice-chairman of Avon Education Committee, objected to the executive's resolution and proposed that the council's view be expressed alternatively in her motion that 'BCRE deplores the fact that an Avon teacher racially abused a fellow teacher. However, it believes that this situation of racial abuse derives from historical factors which in part stem from structural racism in our society and which we are committed to eradicate. In addition, we recognize that Avon is taking steps in a number of ways to combat the problem.' She challenged the portion of the executive's motion which referred to racism at every level, saying that this was not, and could not, be substantiated. She was supported by a head teacher who said that when he saw the executive's resolution it seemed to him like 'a kick in the teeth' and that it was discouraging to teachers who were trying to develop multi-cultural education. The alternative motion was nevertheless defeated by a substantial majority. Shortly afterwards the Pakistan Association issued a press statement repudiating the resolution and declaring their confidence that teachers would 'continue the intellectual argument against racism'.

The debate at the council meeting centred on whether the statements in the executive's resolution were true. Even supposing that they had sufficient evidence to believe them true, it could still have been unwise for them to adopt such a resolution if it detracted from progress towards objectives higher in the list of priorities the council had agreed four years earlier. They said then that the first priority was to ensure the compliance of the local authorities with the requirements of the 1976 act. In considering how they might do that, they had to recognize that virtually all the power to act (to hire and fire staff, declare policy, allocate funds) lay with the authorities. The BCRE could influence the authorities most easily when different bodies or sections of opinion within the authorities were in disagreement; it could then lend its support to another group or coalition. If it decided to make representations it had to consider whether it would be more effective if it made them in private or in public. What it had to avoid was attacking the authority as a whole, unless the issue were exceptional and it wished to appeal to public opinion. In that event the appeal needed to be carefully planned, to try to draw in as many allies as possible and keep the area of criticism very specific. If, as in the case in question, it was seeking a meeting with the authority, it would surely do best to keep its ammunition in reserve and not fire it in advance, because that diminished the chance of obtaining a meeting and weakened the impact of any representations to be made. To adopt a high-profile strategy of proclamation might give some individuals psychological satisfaction but it was to a significant extent playing at symbolic politics instead of husbanding and carefully deploying the rather limited stock of influence at the disposal of a community relations council. The hazard was that an unrealistic strategy sustains expectations that are never met. If a council does not abide by its own scheme of priorities, less is likely to be achieved, there will be more frustration, and members who might otherwise have contributed to the collective effort lose heart and drop out. This is another reason why the output of the race relations industry seems disappointing.

Over the years community relations councils have changed their functions. They started as primarily welfare organizations to help immigrants learn about their rights, the services to which they were entitled, and the procedures by which they could obtain them. Then, since the minorities were not adequately represented in the political and administrative institutions of the country, many councils tried to make up the deficiency by acting as representatives of the minorities. As the minorities' aspirations rose so did their dissatisfactions and the councils tended to take over the assumptions and the rhetoric of the radical philosophy outlined earlier. Their sense of alienation was in many cities deepened by the fears aroused by the proposed legislation which eventually resulted in the British Nationality Act 1981. These fears were often apparent in the course of the Home Affairs Committee's enquiry into Ethnic and Racial Questions in the Census. For example, according to the minutes of evidences when the Chairman of Haringey community relations council, Mrs Hyacinth Moodie, was testifying:

> *Mrs Moodie*: . . . I am talking about young black people born in this country as well.
> *Chairman*: They are British.
> *Mrs Moodie*: Are they British? Since when?
> *Mr Lyon*: Since 1st January 1983.
> *Chairman*: They are British under the Nationality Act.
> *Mrs Moodie*: Perhaps I do not understand.

When Mr Roger Lawrence, Chairman of the West Indian Leadership Council gave evidence there was a similar exchange.

> *Mr Lawrence*: There is no comparison between the United States and this country. We cannot do a comparability study because immigrants in this country can be sent to their country of origin.
> *Mr Lyon*: Do you have a British passport?
> *Mr Lawrence*: Have I got a British passport?
> *Mr Lyon*: Yes.
> *Mr Lawrence*: Yes.
> *Mr Lyon*: You cannot be sent back.
> *Mr Lawrence*: I cannot be sent back?
> *Mr Lyon*: No.
> *Mr Lawrence*: What guarantee can you give me?
> *Mr Lyon*: I can give you an absolute guarantee. There is no right in law to send you back.
> *Mr Lawrence*: Are you sure about that?
> *Mr Lyon*: Absolutely.
> *Mr Lawrence*: We will want you on ransom about that.

The MPs encountered some other hazards in the way of effective communication. For example, in examining Mr G. Virgo, chairman of the Black Parents Pressure Group in Haringey:

> *Mrs Dubs*: Are you saying that being white automatically makes you racist?
>
> *Mr Virgo*: Of course, it is my definition of racist.

What the committee was concerned about, however, was local opposition to a census question which they believed important to their strategy for identifying areas of racial disadvantage and consequent alterations in the allocation of government funds. They found that many people were worried, unnecessarily in the view of the MPs, about the police and government departments getting hold of the confidential information supplied to the census enumerators. These worries had been increased by a campaign conducted when Haringey was selected as a sample area for testing a possible form of question in 1979. For example, a leaflet was circulated headed 'Why we should refuse' stating

> The Government plans new nationality laws . . . They say they need the information to carry out their responsibilities to ethnic minorities. But we know that Government departments are racist (courts, employers, police, etc.). The figures are more likely to be used against us. The information collected will probably find its way to other Government departments. Remember, our homes and addresses will be on the form . . . Say no to the racist census questions. Don't answer questions 10 and 11 on the form.

The approach of the Home Affairs Committee was to try to persuade minority representatives that these fears were groundless, that it was in the interests of the minorities to have such a question, and that they should carry this message back to those whom they represented. Thus:

> *Mr Dubs*: May I put it to the three Councillors that both the Labour Government and this present Conservative Government decided that there would not be an ethnic question in the last Census . . . the three Governments of both parties have been remiss in their attitudes towards the black community . . . If the three of you together go on urging the people who have elected you not to co-operate you could probably sink the Census as far as that is concerned couldn't you?
>
> *Mr Grant*: Yes.

They did not find it easy to persuade them. Thus, in Lewisham:

> *Mr Dubs*: Are you prepared to say to people when the next Census comes along and if there is this sort of question in it, publically, that people have nothing to fear? Individual answers will be

treated confidentially and the purpose of the exercise is to provide benefits for the disadvantaged people in our community. Are you prepared to say that as a politician on a platform?

Mr Gnanapragasam: No, and I will tell you why: because I have not got the necessary confidence that some future administration we have (and we have seen changes – we have seen retrospective laws) will not change. O.K. – it is farfetched, but that is possible, and I am not prepared to stand up.

Likewise in Haringey:

Mr Makanji: I try and represent the electorate . . . their ideas, their fears, their anxieties and all the rest of it. I am not prepared to go in front of them and say 'You should do this.'

And later:

Mr Lyon: What we are saying is that what you did in 1979 was a disservice to your community. You are perfectly entitled to say that is what you thought for yourselves. That does not mean to say that you were right. The mere fact that you are black does not make you right . . . there is no way in which it can militate against you or your children. Certainly not your children because there is no way in which it can be used for immigration purposes against any particular individual.

Mr Lawrence: I will tell you what – in Haringey there is a population of young blacks out there, you go and tell them that it will not militate against them, you go and tell them that. We will not do it, you do it.

There is nothing unusual about the unwillingness of politicians to tell things they know to be true to audiences whom they know will not listen to those things. Nor is there anything unusual about the role of a veto group, a set of people who have the power to block certain kinds of action if they so choose (young blacks in this instance, apparently). What is worth noting, however, is the way minority leaders could be held captive by the fears of their constituents and how many apprehensions could be aroused – reasonably or not – by the various proposals to change the law of nationality.

The problem of the minority representatives was that they could not engage in positive bargaining on behalf of their communities. They could not promise votes or support in return for some undertaking from the MPs, for they command no significant resources that would enable them to put pressure on recalcitrant members of their own groups. This was not always understood. A leading local politician who was involved with the setting up of a community relations committee told the author:

'we looked for leaders'. Members of the majority have looked to those minority members who practised a professional occupation as leaders of their groups, and many minority doctors have indeed served in such a capacity. Otherwise there have been few New Commonwealth minority people who have held the sort of position within the institutional structure of the majority society that has given them a basis for leadership. A minority member with a high-status occupation will be respected by other minority people because they know that majority members will listen to him. Would-be leaders without this advantage can gain support within their own groups by speaking very critically of the majority, but if they are not careful this can weaken their ability to bargain with majority representatives. They can always threaten, but to take a stance unpopular with their more vocal followers required courage. These difficulties can be glimpsed from the exchanges between representatives of the West Indian Standing Conference and the Home Affairs Committee. The representatives were willing to support an ethnic question in the census and to campaign in favour of it, but they had their hesitations and they did not want to lose an opportunity to remind MPs of their grievances, suspicions and apprehensions. They did not want to be confined to just the one point on which they were going to make what might seem to some of their supporters like a concession. Thus:

> Mr Charles: Only when you accept the starting point of a black presence as part of the socio-economic political structure of the society which at this point you are not putting into practice then will we begin to see that you are genuinely prepared to accept an ethnical question to do something about it . . .
>
> Mr Hunt: If you had studied the work and record of this Sub-Committee I think you would realize that we indeed do accept the presence of black people in Britain and we are concerned to improve their lot. What I am saying to you is that if you persist in the sort of attitude and chip-on-the-shoulder approach which you have shown here this morning you will deter the Government from ever doing anything so far as a Census question is concerned. We shall be forced to recommend that there is no point in going ahead with this because of the opposition from the black community . . .
>
> Mr Charles: . . . You have failed because you are looking down and speaking down to black people and telling us how to behave . . . we want a partnership situation . . . ask us for advice and we will give it to you . . . when we are genuinely sure that you are really interested in putting it into practice.
>
> Mr Lyon: Do you think that the black community is disadvantaged?
>
> Mr Trant: I am asking you.

That last exchange of question and question is an important indicator of the structure within which, at present, any negotiations have to recur. The minority spokesmen want to ask the questions: they sense that otherwise they cannot put on the agenda the matters of concern to them because the whole administrative machine operates on a basis which does not provide for ethnic representation. It is difficult to build a partnership relation when all the power is on one side.

Another difficulty is that in stressing how much remains to be done both minority leaders and people from the majority involved in community relations have tended to overlook or disparage some of the achievements of recent years. To quote some further evidence from Haringey:

> *Mr Hunt:* The point I am trying to make is that *bona fides* of this Committee is reasonably good in this sphere in that we are drawing Parliamentary and public attention to the problems of the minority communities in a way which has not been done previously. You do not acknowledge that?
>
> *Mr Grant:* I am prepared to accept that this Committee has brought a number of situations to the attention of Parliament, yes, and for example if what you say in terms of the monitoring in the civil service was done by your Committee – I thought it had been thrown out by government – if that is so then clearly the Committee has made some impact in Parliament, yes.
>
> *Chairman:* This Committee recommended the repeal of the sus law and achieved that. Do you remember that?
>
> *Mr Grant:* Yes.

In the 'liberal hour' of 1965–8 the tone of discussions about community relations was set by white liberals in positions of influence. The note was optimistic. The source of the difficulties was identified as white prejudice and discrimination and these, it was thought, could be significantly reduced within a decade or two. Fifteen years later the tone of discussion is set by the people, of all complexions, who deal with the problems of race relations on a day-to-day basis and are frustrated by the slow pace of progress. The note is pessimistic. The source of the difficulties is said to be a racism rooted in centuries of British history and manifested in all institutions of British society. It is made to sound so formidable a foe that the faint-hearted are inclined to give up. The radicals who insist that little can be achieved without comprehensive social change must bear some of the responsibility for the mood of depression. Had they more pride in the achievements of the past fifteen years and more confidence in future progress, community relations workers could communicate better with the public, of all sections, and their work would be more productive.

7

Conclusion

In the Preface the question was asked: why has the output of the race relations industry seemed so disappointing in relation to the input into it? Six kinds of answer were then listed. In retrospect it can be seen that underneath the answers lie different assumptions about what public policy can achieve. The answers overlap in various ways, but the second, fourth and fifth answers blame particular groups for a lack of progress: the staff of community relations bodies for not doing a better job; the government for lack of vision and commitment, and parliament for failing to exert sufficient corrective influence upon the government. These answers presume that in other circumstances much more progress could have been made. The other answers maintain that it would be unrealistic to expect official policies to have had a much more substantial effect upon everyday conduct. A great deal depends upon changes in the expectations of ethnic minority members; upon their ability to inter-relate with majority members, and upon their becoming better acquainted with them. It takes time, too, to identify appropriate goals for public policy in this area and to create institutional means for attaining them. Some of the differences between the answers that ascribe blame and those that stress constraints can be traced to the varying conceptions of the relation between the individual and society discussed in Chapter 1.

Underlying the presentation of these issues has been the claim that majority–minority relations and the policy process can both usefully be seen in terms of bargaining. Majority and minority members alike seek their objectives and either make deals or refuse them; in the course of time they come to bargain more effectively. One of the tasks of public policy is to expedite this development and, by preventing the exploitation of the weaker parties, to regulate it. Seen from this standpoint it is necessary to pause before accepting any claim that the achievements of the race relations industry have been disappointing, not because there have been no disappointments – for clearly there have been – but because the so-called industry is not an organization of producers selling something that consumers can buy if they like. It does not manufacture a private good. The people who are said to belong to the race relations industry are appointed to help maximize the public welfare. An employer who engages or promotes a worker on grounds of race rather than ability damages that welfare, for the accumulation of minor acts of discrimination adds up to a major social evil. The prime tasks are to identify what is at fault and to assess the effectiveness of alternative remedies. If some of those who have tried to remedy matters have done a bad job it is necessary to work out what should have been done instead. The achievements of community relations workers in the reduction of racial discrimination should be assessed along lines similar to the evaluation of the work of environmental health officers in reducing the risks of disease.

When mass immigration from the New Commonwealth got under way in the late 1950s it was the short-term problems that attracted attention. The migrants were admitted to take the jobs the natives did not want. The British (like the Germans, the French, and other European nations which made similar use of migrant labour) did not foresee that their society would have to change as a consequence. As the whites under-estimated the long-term implications of the migration, so they under-estimated how much would have to be done to alleviate the social problems associated with it. The immigrants, on their side, were quite unable to foresee all the consequences of the steps they were taking. They were aware of their disappointments but under-estimated the extent of the changes necessary, on both sides, to attain a greater measure of equality.

In industrial relations the two sides bargain primarily about how hard people are to work and what share they are to receive of the proceeds. In race relations the bargaining is about how much people on the two sides are to change their ways. It may be a matter of one side giving up something (like a discriminatory practice) for the benefit of the other, which would be a zero-sum bargain. In so far as the whole society benefits from greater racial harmony this will be a positive-sum bargain. Since the incentives to change include threats as well as rewards there is always the possibility that, on balance, everyone will be worse off as a result of a conflict and this will be a negative-sum bargain. The incentives for the minority members to adopt majority practices are partly financial, in that by learning the language and customs of the majority they qualify for better-paid jobs. Their response to these incentives will depend substantially upon their expectations of the future. If they expect to settle in their new country, and expect their children to grow up there they may change their ways in the interest of their children. As was suggested in Chapter 4, whether they think an incentive sufficient to justify a change will depend upon how attached they are to the values of the country from which they have come and upon their feelings about their new country. Immigrant minorities which are not physically distinguishable will find it easier to change than racial minorities. Members of the latter may think it not worthwhile changing if there is a constant threat of rebuff. Where there are racial differences members of the dominant group are apt to judge members of the subordinate group alike, according to their colour rather than their conduct. The changes which are demanded of members of the majority, if their society is to incorporate on terms of equality a racial minority, are greater than the changes required in respect of a minority that is not physically distinguishable.

The members of some minorities are more attached than others to homeland customs and therefore require a greater incentive to make them change their ways. Asians have stronger homeland ties than West Indians but the position is more complicated because of the extent to which Asians have succeeded in transplanting homeland cultures to Britain. If a young Sikh hesitates between British and Sikh norms about, say, friendship with people of the opposite sex before marriage, the relevant Sikh norms will be those which obtain among the Sikh community in that part of Britain where the young person lives, not the traditional norms in the Punjab. Because the Sikhs have established their own communal institutions in Britain they may be less likely to think of returning permanently to their homelands than West Indians, though the cultural gap between the West Indians and the English is smaller than that between the Sikhs and the English.

Differences of age may also be relevant. The longer the migrant stays in the new country the more he or she may become attached to that country's ways, even though a few may in their old age prefer to return to the land of their birth. Among the majority it is probable that older people may be less tolerant of minority customs and less ready to change their ways to suit the wishes of the newcomers.

Thus there is a kind of bargaining situation with, on the one hand, a large majority divided among themselves about the kind of deal they should offer to the minority. On the other, there is a collection of ethnic

minorities, each one divided within itself about the demands to be made
of the majority and the strengths of its investment either in the prospect
of return to the homeland or in a distinctive community based upon a
transplanted culture. Small numbers of political activists drawn from all
the minorities come together periodically in the attempt to organize a
bargaining agency for all minorities, but these attempts have hitherto
been very short lived. There will be bargaining between individuals
within the minorities and majority, and, occasionally, by associations
acting on behalf of one or more minorities when local circumstances
make this possible, but experience shows that any expectations of
bargaining between ethnic groups will be frustrated. Some members of
the majority believe that if it were possible for representatives of the
majority and minority to strike a bargain about the commitment of
minority members to British institutions this could provide a better
foundation for future policy. Thus when the Home Affairs Committee
was drafting its report on racial disadvantage Mr William Waldegrave
MP proposed an amendment such that part of the document would have
read: 'It is not unfair for the old communities of the United Kingdom to
expect allegiance to be whole-heartedly transferred to the immigrants'
new nation, in exchange for the proper commitment of the host
communities to total acceptance of the newcomers as full and equal
citizens of the United Kingdom.' He later withdrew his proposal,
perhaps because it did not find favour with his colleagues; after all, a
general declaration like this has little practical effect. The transfer of
allegiance comes about gradually and often imperceptibly unlike, say,
the transfer of rights to property. Nevertheless, Waldegrave's amendment does grasp one of the main causes of the uncertainty felt by many
people on both sides of the colour line about the best course of action to
follow.

   Many of the situations of racial and ethnic relations that have been
studied by social scientists have been ones in which none of the main
parties had anywhere else to go. That is why many of them, like the
Afrikaners in South Africa, have felt that they had their backs to the wall
and needed to struggle with determination. Most of the Europeans who
went to America, North and South, from the seventeenth century
onwards, either travelled with the intention of settling there or soon
decided against return to their countries of origin. The Africans who
were taken to the Americas had no option; nor did most of the refugee
groups. They had to plan their lives in America on the assumption that
they and their descendants would be buried there. The native popula-

tion, consisting of Amerindians and the descendants of earlier settlers, knew that the newcomers were there to stay; the institutions of the native societies, like in the United States the rules about what immigrants had to do to qualify for citizenship, allowed for a continuing influx of new settlers.

It has been very different in Britain, and in consequence the situation there is characterized by a relatively high level of uncertainty on the part of both the minorities and the majority. The uncertainties of the immigrants and their descendants have contributed to the uncertainties of the natives and these have added to the uncertainties of the first group in an interactive process. Since it is necessary to start somewhere, and since the uncertainties are greatest for the minority members, their position can be considered first.

The first wave of immigrants were mainly sojourners, that is, migrants (mostly male) who came to Britain to obtain paid employment, save money, and return, but who never kept to their plan and stayed on from one decade to the next while continuing to think of themselves as temporary residents. This process gives rise to 'the myth of return': people talk of going back and the possibility remains important psychologically to them, but the likelihood of their doing so progressively diminishes. So long as the myth is maintained they do not organize their lives to best advantage within their new societies. Another source of uncertainty lies in the majority society. Politicians have made speeches advocating that New Commonwealth immigrants be repatriated; so long as that seems a possibility (and the Asians, at least, will remember what happened in East Africa) it seems advisable to keep open an escape route, both materially and psychologically. Thus some of the Asian minorities expelled from East Africa now have kinsfolk in Canada, Britain, India, and in the states around the Arabian Gulf, who sustain a network of mutual aid that could be important in the event of trouble. Their commitment to Britain is less than that of people who have no escape route. The majority society has also of late been suffering from an economic recession: jobs are scarce, and therefore racial discrimination is the more to be feared. Some may conclude that Britain cannot offer good long-term economic prospects to members of its ethnic minorities.

The minority member who contemplates possible trends in majority attitudes is drawn to the sort of opinions discussed in Chapter 1. Are majority sentiments determined by deeply rooted feelings of racial solidarity and antipathy? For if so then either the long-term prospect is bleak or the only hope depends upon the minorities' organizing and challenging every disclosure of prejudice, for they will not be able to rely upon the majority's policies and procedures. If majority sentiments are thought to be determined by feelings of nationalism, or of class struggle, or to be the outcome of a jumble of multifarious influences, then in each case other implications follow. Perhaps the bleakest inference is that drawn by the Rastafarians who liken British society to that of Babylon for it is the city of their captivity. Their myth of return is of return not to the Caribbean but to Africa, and since there is little chance of this becoming a reality the Rastafarians' view of their predicament turns in upon itself and offers no adequate programme of escape from Babylon.

The argument of this book has been that the Race Relations Acts of 1965 and 1968 were a recognition that racial harmony is a public good. The motivation behind them was quite different from that behind the United States acts of 1964, 1965 and 1968. They were not forced from parliament by freedom rides, marches and assassinations after three centuries of legally sanctioned racial discrimination. Though there were many hesitations and some reluctance, these were non-party measures passed because discrimination was seen as contrary to the British people's conception of themselves and their society. The effect of the acts was sustained, to a far greater extent than has ever been the case in the United States, by a national system of health, housing and other welfare benefits administered on a colour-blind basis. Within the framework of the British Empire, West Indians, South Asians and others had acquired British nationality and features of British culture which gave them a status within the metropolitan countries that few migrant workers in other European countries enjoyed (excepting only the Netherlands). People of New Commonwealth origin settled in Britain as British subjects and although Pakistan left the Commonwealth in 1972 her nationals in Britain have not been put at any significant disadvantage because of that. The incidence of racial prejudice and discrimination has been documented, but there has been growing recognition of its extent and seriousness. Discrimination has not prevented some minority members from becoming successful figures in British public and commercial life. So it is not surprising if many minority members believe that prospects for them are better in Britain than any other country in which they might live.

The uncertainty attaches to the position of minority people as members of groups. Life in Britain offers opportunities, but these are often conditional upon their conforming to British expectations. When in Rome, do as the Romans – or so it is said. Many, perhaps most, minority members are unwilling to try to conform as individuals, so long as they are physically identified as belonging in a separate and disfavoured category. Their group identity is a valued source of support which it would be premature to discard. So a major source of uncertainty centres upon the question: 'if we stay in Britain what collective strategy should we follow?' Asians can say to themselves: 'in East Africa we built up separate communities; this was ultimately to our disadvantage, but who knows if any other strategy would have been better?' (It is not suggested that people ask themselves such questions explicitly, but that an awareness of their importance underlies other discussions of the best lines of action for individuals and families in the course of their daily lives.) Even if members of a minority could agree upon a preferred strategy they might not be able to carry it out because other members of their minority do not share their values and can block their plan. Thus Chapter 4 described how Sikh men who had compromised with British customs and did not wear turbans at work were obliged to support turban protests and to fall in line with more traditional community expectations. A study of Sikhs in Gravesend described how life for the children changed when their aunts arrived and the balance of power within the community tipped in favour of the traditionalists (Helweg, 1979: 55). Among the Asian minorities of East Africa the Ismailis were the most westernized and they were encouraged by their leader, the Aga Khan, to adapt to the changing opportunities for employment presented by the West. So the fi_st young Ismaili men and women to settle in London adopted English customs and attitudes. When others from East Africa joined them and recreated an Ismaili community, the modernizers were pulled back and obliged to conform more to minority norms.

The majority offers minority members rewards for conforming to majority expectations. Whether minority people think the rewards sufficient for it to be worthwhile for them to conform, will depend in part upon the value they place upon what they have to give up. They will find it more difficult to estimate the long-term implications of their decisions than the short, and it will not be surprising if in these circumstances people prefer an alternative which offers a moderate reward with security to a high reward with substantial risk. In a culture oriented to a zero-sum conception of group competition (as most of the Asian minorities have been) and with experience of threatening behaviour by a majority which has led to their being robbed of their savings and expelled from the country, many people will see their ethnic community as offering a moral and material security superior to anything the ethnic majority can promise. Their responses can be interpreted as a form of decision-making under conditions of uncertainty. Perhaps it is as well to stress that uncertainty can also be seen as a kind of middle range in-between the spheres of anticipated positive and negative reward. If minority members were sure that their best strategy was to Anglicize themselves as quickly as possible there would be no uncertainty. Equally there would be no uncertainty if they were sure that all they could expect was hostility. The situation of ethnic minorities in Britain in the 1970s was neither so hopeful that minority members felt they could dispense with collective organization, nor so hopeless that they were impelled to create effective agencies to coordinate their struggles.

There are, therefore, grounds for seeing minority behaviour as a reflection of the uncertainties of their situation. There are also grounds for seeing majority attitudes as influenced by uncertainty. The settlement of New Commonwealth immigrants presented novel problems for the English. No policy prescription appeared to hold out much hope of solving these problems and those that were advanced (often in very general terms) seemed certain to excite white resentment. Since there was no recognized solution, it seemed best to deal with the short-term difficulties and wait until the situation was clarified.

The views which white people held about likely long-term developments are associated with the philosophies outlined in Chapter 1. Some think that racial differences create constraints beyond the reach of social policies. Others believe that the prospects of improving relations depend upon the willingness of the minority to identify themselves with British nationality. Yet others maintain that ethnic and racial conflict will eventually be swept up in more comprehensive class conflicts. These, of course, are not the only possible views of the character of British society. Some consider that it is best understood as a 'mass society', one in which the media of mass communications are of particular importance; in which much behaviour is oriented to patterns of mass consumption; and in which inter-group relations are fashioned by the same influences as those which bear upon individual consumers.

Chapters 5 and 6 have described the difficulties which race relations agencies have experienced in trying to establish priorities. These difficulties surely reflect a wider uncertainty about the character of a general policy for promoting racial harmony. From the standpoint of the majority many of the problems are brought together in the popular conception of assimilation. Should the majority make their plans on the assumption that the minorities will gradually lose their distinctiveness or not? Will differences of skin colour have lost most of their significance by the third generation? More difficult still, since the majority have some power to influence the outcome, do they want the minorities to lose or retain their distinctiveness? It is impossible to write confidently about these questions since they were scarcely ever discussed explicitly, but underlying the attitudes of many majority members in the 1950s and 1960s was an assumption that ethnic minority members would want gradually to become culturally British. When, later, minority representatives denied this and said that they wished to retain their distinctiveness, the majority were confused. They could see that in a great variety of ways minority members were certain to come to resemble the majority more closely. In what ways would they remain distinct? Those people who have spoken for multi-cultural education (mostly white radicals and liberals) have added to the confusion by advocating solutions such as that of 'cultural pluralism' without being able to describe with sufficient clarity just what this solution would be and how it could be implemented. It might have been better had they based their arguments upon the value which has been placed in British history upon the toleration of religious and political dissent, and upon the sensitivity to cultural variation which was cultivated in a classical education (for many besides the author must once have learned about such variation by studying the differences between ancient Athens and Sparta). Had they stressed the importance of these themes in the national tradition and indicated ways of extending them to contemporary problems their audience would have felt they were on more familiar ground and a more coherent philosophy of education for this field might have emerged.

If the line of analysis employed in this book is valid, then the uncertainty about majority–minority relations in Britain can be expected to continue but probably diminish. People from both sides of the dividing line can be expected to go on looking to central government to reduce the uncertainty by formulating an authoritative policy, but since there is little prospect of any such policy commanding wide support, all that is certain is, on the one hand, a series of general exhortations, and, on the other, of minor innovations and readjustments to respond to small-scale problems. Dissatisfaction with the so-called race relations industry will continue because the people who are seen as employees or volunteers in that industry cannot dispel the uncertainties generated by the broader structure of social relations.

It looks as if the National Committee on Commonwealth Immigrants was right to insist that local community relations councils should exist not to serve the interests of one section of the population but to promote racial harmony and be beneficial to all. Minority spokesmen who are unable to create effective minority organizations have often wanted to take over the official structure to make it serve their interests. If they were ever able to do so, that structure would not be able to claim the same support from public funds. There would be an argument for creating some new kind of council in which minority representatives could then discuss problems with representatives of majority institutions (some of whom could well, in their personal capacities, be members of the ethnic minorities too). A better course is for voluntary associations among the ethnic minorities, as among the majority, to be seen as representing only those who are actual members of the associations. All individuals should be free to identify themselves as they wish; ideally they should not be assigned to any section of the population with which they do not identify. The Commission for Racial Equality and the local councils are institutions of a white society that now includes a sprinkling of non-white individuals who hold posts in that society's institutions. The Commission and the councils need to speak to that white society, emphasizing that racial discrimination is contrary to the society's ethical ideals and its law. They need to organize so as to make maximum use of the law by seeing that discrimination is challenged and the judgements of the courts are brought to the attention of those affected by them. It is sometimes said that the suppression of discrimination does not eradicate sentiments of prejudice in the minds of discriminators, but there is good reason to believe that much expressed prejudice is to be understood as stemming from the pressure individuals feel to conform to what they believe to be the social norms prevailing in the groups to which they belong or seek to belong. If actual patterns of behaviour are changed by legal regulation, this gradually changes group norms and the pressures of conformity then operate so as to induce people to conform to the new norms. The laws against racial discrimination are of incomparable importance in reducing uncertainty about the proper ways of conducting inter-racial relations and they must provide the central thrust of any policy to promote racial harmony.

For a period of twenty years, from the Commonwealth Immigration Act of 1962 until the coming into effect of the Nationality Act 1981, questions of harmony between people assigned to different racial groups in Britain have been confounded with the questions surrounding New Commonwealth immigration. Immigration controls have had a very unsettling effect upon the Asian minorities. As a Haringey councillor told the Home

Affairs Committee 'there is not a single Asian family in this country who have not had one of their family or one of their friends actually stopped and questioned at length at Heathrow or Gatwick or any other port of entry'. The nationality legislation – as the previous chapter illustrated – has upset people of Caribbean as well as South Asian origin, but there should now be no further occasion for doubt about entitlement to reside in Britain without fear of deportation. In 1971 West Indian immigration came to an end and primary immigration from the Indian subcontinent terminated before the end of the twenty-year period. White people have no reason to fear any further wave of immigration. This could be a good moment for the government to open a new era by demonstrating a real commitment to action against discrimination in employment. In a more settled atmosphere it should be possible to emphasize shared values, to help people concentrate on realistic objectives and, by allowing them to take pride in what has already been achieved, enable them to be more confident about promoting racial harmony.

Bibliography

Abbott, Simon (ed.), 1971, The Prevention of Racial Discrimination in Britain. London: Oxford University Press.

Atkinson, A. B., Maynard, A. K. and Trinder, C. G., 1983, Parents and Children: Incomes in Two Generations. London: Heinemann.

Bailey, F. G., 1965, Decisions by Consensus in Councils and Committees: With Special Reference to Village and Local Government in India, in Michael Banton (ed.), Political Systems and the Distribution of Power, pp. 1–20. (ASA monographs, 2) London: Tavistock Publications.

Bagehot, Walter, 1873, Physics and Politics, or Thoughts on the Application of the Principles of 'Natural Selection' and 'Inheritance' to Political Society. London: Kegan Paul edition of 1905.

Ballard, Roger and Ballard, Catherine, 1977, The Sikhs: The Development of South Asian Settlements in Britain, in James Watson (ed.), Between Two Cultures; Migrants and Minorities in Britain, pp. 2–56. Oxford: Blackwell.

Banton, Michael, 1955, The Coloured Quarter: Negro Immigrants in a Dockland Area. London: Cape.

　1972, Racial Minorities. London: Fontana.

　1983, Racial and Ethnic Competition. Cambridge: Cambridge University Press.

Barker, Anthony, 1975, Strategy and Style in Local Community Relations. Prepared for the Runnymede Trust and submitted to the House of Commons Select Committee on Race Relations and Immigration. London.

Beetham, David, 1970, Transport and Turbans; A comparative Study in Local Politics. London: Oxford University Press.

Benyon, John (ed.), 1984, Scarman and After: Essays reflecting on Lord Scarman's Report, the Riots and their Aftermath. Oxford: Pergamon.

Crewe, Ivor, 1983, Representation and the Ethnic Minorities in Britain, in Nathan Glazer and Ken Young (eds.), Ethnic Pluralism and Public Policy: Achieving Equality in the United States and Britain, pp. 258–84. London: Heinemann, and Lexington, MA: DC Heath.

Dahya, Badr, 1981, Correspondence. New Community, 9: 111–12.

Dummett, Michael and Dummett, Ann, 1969, The Role of Government in Britain's Racial Crisis, in Lewis Donnelly (ed.), Justice First, pp. 25–78. London: Sheed and Ward.

Gaskell, George, and Smith, Patten, 1981, 'Alienated' Black Youth: an investigation of 'Conventional Wisdom' Explanations, New Community, 9: 182–93.

132

Glazer, Nathan, 1975, *Affirmative Discrimination: Ethnic Inequality and Public Policy*. 2nd edn 1978. New York: Basic Books.

Glazer, Nathan, and Moynihan, Daniel Patrick, 1975, *Ethnicity: Theory and Experience*. Cambridge, MA: Harvard University Press.

Hall, Phoebe; Land, Hilary; Parker, Roy and Webb, Adrian, 1975, *Change, Choice and Conflict in Social Policy*. London: Heinemann.

Harsanyi, John C., 1982, Morality and the Theory of Rational Behaviour, in Sen, Amartya and Williams, Bernard (eds.), *Utilitarianism and Beyond*, pp. 39–62. Cambridge: Cambridge University Press.

Hechter, Michael; Friedman, Debra and Appelbaum, Malka, 1982, A Theory of Ethnic Collective Action. *International Migration Review*, 16: 412–34.

Heineman, Benjamin W., Jr, 1972, *The Politics of the Powerless: A study of the Campaign Against Racial Discrimination*. London: Oxford University Press.

Helweg, Arthur H., 1979, *Sikhs in England: The Development of a Migrant Community*. Delhi: Oxford University Press.

Hill, Michael J., and Issacharoff, Ruth, 1971, *Community Action and Race Relations: A Study of Community Relations Committees in Britain*. London: Oxford University Press.

Hirschmann, Albert O., 1970, *Exit, Voice and Loyalty*. Cambridge, MA: Harvard University Press.

Jeffery, Patricia, 1976, *Migrants and Refugees: Muslim and Christian Pakistani Families in Bristol*. Cambridge: Cambridge University Press.

Katznelson, Ira, 1973, *Black Men, White Cities: Race, Politics, and Migration in the United States, 1900–30, and Britain, 1948–68*. London: Oxford University Press.

Keith, Sir Arthur, 1931, *The Place of Prejudice in Modern Civilization*. London: Williams and Norgate.

Killian, Lewis M., 1979, 'The Race Relations Industry as a Sensitizing Concept. *Research in Social Problems in Public Policy*, 1: 113–37.

Kosmin, Barry A. and Levy, Caren, 1983, *Jewish Identity in an Anglo-Jewish Community*. London: Board of Deputies of British Jews.

Martin, Bernice, 1981, *A Sociology of Contemporary Cultural Change*. Oxford: Blackwell.

Miles, Robert, 1982, *Racism and Migrant Labour*. London: Routledge.

Olson, Mancur, 1965, *The Logic of Collective Action: Public Goods and the Theory of Groups*. Cambridge, MA: Harvard University Press.

Patterson, Sheila, 1968, *Immigration and Race Relations in Britain 1960–1967*. London: Oxford University Press.

Radcliffe, Lord, 1969, Immigration and Settlement: Some General Considerations, *Race*, 11: 35–51.

Reddaway, John, 1970, Whatever Happened to the Community Relations Commission? *Race Today*, July, 213–15.

Rose, E. J. B., *et al.*, 1969, *Colour and Citizenship: A Report on British Race Relations*. London: Oxford University Press.

van den Berghe, Pierre L., 1981, *The Ethnic Phenomenon*. Amsterdam: Elsevier.

Index